The
Little Black
Book for Guys

The Little Black Book for Guys

Guys Talk About Sex

by Youth for Youth

St. Stephen's Community House

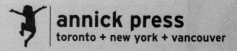

annick press
toronto + new york + vancouver

This book contains general reference information about sexuality and health issues. It is not intended as a substitute for the advice of a trained medical professional. Readers should not attempt to diagnose or treat themselves based on material contained in this book, but rather should consult an appropriate medical professional before starting or stopping any medication and before implementing any other treatment discussed in this book. The authors and publisher are not responsible for any adverse effects resulting from the information contained in this book.

© 2008 St. Stephen's Community House (text and illustrations)

Annick Press Ltd.

We acknowledge the support of the Canada Council for the Arts, the Ontario Arts Council, and the Government of Canada through the Book Publishing Industry Development Program (BPIDP) for our publishing activities.

 Canada Council   Conseil des Arts   ONTARIO ARTS COUNCIL
for the Arts   du Canada   CONSEIL DES ARTS DE L'ONTARIO

Cataloging in Publication

The little black book for guys : guys talk about sex / St. Stephen's Community House.

Includes index.
ISBN 978-1-55037-962-4

1. Sex instruction for boys—Juvenile literature. 2. Teenage boys—Sexual behavior—Juvenile literature. 3. Teenage boys—Health and hygiene—Juvenile literature. I. St. Stephen's Community House (Toronto, Ont.) II. Title.

HQ41.L58 2008   j613.9'53   C2008-904286-7

Distributed in Canada by:	Published in the U.S.A. by Annick Press (U.S.) Ltd.
Firefly Books Ltd.	Distributed in the U.S.A. by:
66 Leek Crescent	Firefly Books (U.S.) Inc.
Richmond Hill, ON	P.O. Box 1338
L4B 1H1	Ellicott Station
	Buffallo, NY 14205

Printed and bound in Canada.

Visit us at: www.annickpress.com

CONTENTS

Preface   vii

Introduction   x

Chapter 1   1
  LOVE MACHINE: THE PENIS

Chapter 2   27
  MAKING THE CONNECTION: RELATIONSHIPS

Chapter 3   81
  LET'S GET IT ON: SEX

Chapter 4   137
  THE THIN RED LINE: HIV/AIDS AND OTHER
  SEXUALLY TRANSMITTED INFECTIONS

Chapter 5   185
  TAKING CONTROL: BIRTH CONTROL

Resources   225

Glossary   232

About St. Stephen's   238

Acknowledgments   239

Index   241

Preface

I had to become a man at a really young age. Being an immigrant and not living with my parents had a huge impact on how I grew up, my opinions of men around me, and what I believed manhood to be. I had to look to other men in the community to help me learn and grow—some of the attitudes I absorbed were healthy and some were certainly not. When you are in search of something, sometimes you can end up with the incorrect information or fall in with an unhealthy mentor.

I ended up piecing together ideas of what it meant to be a man from lots of places: music, TV, men on the block, and most importantly, my women friends. I wish that, when I was a teenager, I could have been around more men who talked honestly about manhood, sex, and relationships. I wish I had had a book like the one you're holding in your hands.

This book came into being thanks to the St. Stephen's Community House Youth Arcade. The Arcade is a youth drop-in center in downtown Toronto. It's a place where you can be yourself—with all the good, the bad, and the ugly that is you—and nobody is going to judge you. It is also a place that encourages you to challenge your assumptions, to think critically about the world around you, and to contribute what you can to the community. It was through the Arcade that, a few years ago, a group of young women put together *The Little Black Book for Girlz: A Book on Healthy Sexuality*. The book was a hit.

Thanks to the girls' success, the Arcade became a place where young men also started to talk about sex in a non-judgmental, honest way. We began to meet weekly as a group and shared our experiences, a lot of laughs, and the particular problems we faced as young men. Eventually, the group became such a supportive network that we decided to collect material for our own book: *The Little Black Book for Guys*. We wanted a book that, like our group, could help guys bridge the gap between the world's expectations of us and what we were actually experiencing.

When we first started writing, all our machismo came out. We wanted to sound like (and be thought of as) people with answers, people with solutions, and yet not like the other "guys"—you know, the loudmouth dogs of the bunch. It took some time for us to admit that we didn't have all the answers, we weren't experts, and we weren't perfect. What we did have was our experiences, and we've tried to write about them honestly. You will see that this is a book of many voices, cultures, and perspectives. We tried not to focus on "right or wrong" but just what's real. When information required an expert, we talked to one; in fact, health professionals have read through everything to make sure we didn't mess up any facts. We hope you find answers to your questions about sex and relationships, but no book can cover everything. That's why we've included a list of resources at the back. There you'll find a bunch of websites and phone numbers that can help you get the answers you need.

This book is an example of what can happen when young men are honest, free to be themselves, and given the opportunity to share their experiences and ideas. Our hope is that you will use this book to help you make informed decisions, to think about your own experiences, and to share more honestly with other guys so they can also become healthy men, balanced boyfriends, and excellent fathers. No book can tell you who you are, but we hope this book helps you find your own comfortable definition of what it means to be a man.

Happy reading!

Marlon Merraro, *Manager, Youth Services*
St. Stephen's Community House

INTRODUCTION

Welcome to THE LITTLE BLACK BOOK…*FOR GUYS*!

Yeah, okay, so the girls beat us to it. Somewhere out there, at a bookstore near you, there's a little something called *The Little Black Book for Girlz*. It's a bunch of writing and interviews and poems and pictures that was put together by an impressive group of girls right here at St. Stephen's Community House. They wanted to be in the driver's seat when it came to expressing their thoughts and questions about sex, and the book they made is one sweet ride.

But now it's our turn to drive. What you got here is a book that was put together mostly by young men who've spent time at St. Stephen's Youth Arcade. Hanging out with each other, and with our main man Marlon Merraro and our number one guy Gordon McLean who helped run the drop-in program, we realized that guys have their own issues and questions about sex. Problem is we don't spend a lot time talking about it with each other. Well that's bullshit! It's the 21st century. We figured: here we were living in downtown Toronto—one of the most diverse cities in the world—with every kind of person you could talk to, but we weren't talking. If *we* weren't, chances are, a lot of guys out there weren't either.

So we started talking. We made lists of stuff we wanted to know or discuss. We talked about stuff we'd been through person-ally—relationships, sex, even getting girls pregnant. And you know what? Hearing about this stuff is a lot more interesting coming from a real guy your own age than from some public health pamphlet. That's why we started to write this stuff down. Some of it we worked on as a group. Some of us had personal stories to tell. All of it began to pile up, and the next thing we knew (yeah... two years later!), we had ourselves a book. And now you have yourself a book.

Enough of the origin story. You want to get to the good stuff. So read on, and when you're done reading, pass it on to one of your guy friends. Better yet, talk to him about it.

Peace out,

The Group

LOVE MACHINE
The Penis

CHAPTER 1

Head and Shoulders, Knees and Toes...

Welcome to Chapter 1... Yes, that is a very boring way to introduce a chapter, which COULD lead to the assumption that the chapter is really boring—but you are deceived, my friend! For this chapter is all about a body part that I know you don't find boring: your penis.

We've all had adventures with our friend Mr. Dick. Have you ever been to a school dance and worked up the nerve to dance with that special someone—only to have your little friend ruin it by getting hard so that you felt like you had to leave a foot of space between you or else your dance partner would think you were a total perve? Even worse, ever been picked to talk at the front of the class and then realized that your little friend was trying to say hello? Or how about waking up from a hot dream to find your bed sheets wet—and not from piss. A lot of guys are like "What the hell is this? No one told me about this! Why wasn't I warned?"

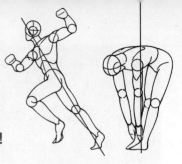

We all know that our bodies are changing—that's not news. But, do you know why, when, where, who, and what is changing about it? Well, mi amigo, you've come to the right chapter. Most girls are taught about their periods before they have them, but guys aren't always told about the ups and downs of having a penis.

Well, this chapter is here to tell you all about how your body works, especially your penis. That's right, we're going on a penis tour. Knowing how your body works inside and out, and knowing that other guys are experiencing exactly the same stuff that you are, makes having a penis a whole lot easier to deal with.

So buckle up and get ready to unzip the crazy world of the penis!

Boys II Men
(like the band...but not)
PUBERTY

Andrew Coimbra

Puberty. We all go through it, male or female. The fact is that it's part of life. The grossness, the changes, the pimples, the "new feelings"—all that crap. It's just one of those things that happens to you whether you like it or not, so why not polish up on your knowledge so you can be smart about what's coming (so to speak) or happening right now?

So when does it start? Different ages for different people, but generally guys experience puberty between ages 10 and 18. Puberty kicks into gear when your body starts cranking out certain types of hormones (stuff your cells make that tells other cells how to grow). For guys, the main hormone is testosterone (for girls, it's estrogen). Testosterone gets your body's sex equipment into working order (congratulations! you can now get a girl pregnant!), but that's not all it does...

Testosterone also causes your body to start looking (and sounding) like a man, which is why you don't get any love from girls until puberty hits, amigo. Here are some of those manly physical changes:

- **taller height:** Guys go through a growth spurt of usually about 10 cm (4 inches) a year.

- **deeper voice:** Guys experience a voice change, a deepening that is due to the thickening of vocal chords. (cool, eh?)
- **hairy face, pits, and balls:** Facial hair begins to grow. Hair appears in the underarms and pubic hair grows around the genitals. The hair gradually becomes thicker.
- **bigger man stuff:** Shoulders broaden, muscle development increases, and the penis and testicles grow significantly. (oh, yeah!)
- **bigger breasts:** Huh? For guys?? Yup. During puberty, it is common for guys to develop temporary breast enlargement (it's called gynaecomastia—look it up if you don't believe me). Key word: temporary. It goes away within the span of two years—so no worries, you're not turning into a girl.

Anything else? Yeah. Testosterone will also cause your dick to get hard (erections) more often, your balls to make sperm (the stuff in cum—semen—that can make a girl pregnant), and maybe even make you cum while you're sleeping. Keep reading for more about all this stuff.

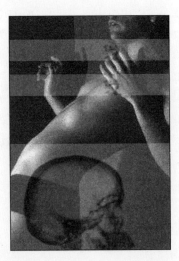

Uh-Oh; Delayed Puberty

Andrew Coimbra

Guys go through puberty at different ages, generally in the years between 10 and 18. By the time you're 15, though, puberty should probably have started. If you are 15 and there are no signs that testosterone has started doing its thing (check out the list on the previous pages), it may be "delayed puberty."

Don't panic—it happens. Puberty could be delayed for any of these reasons:

- It might be a family thing: Maybe the people in your family are simply late bloomers. That means your delayed puberty is a genetic thing, known as constitutional delay, which is cool because you probably don't require any treatments—your hormones are just taking their time before they kick in. Check with your doctor to be sure.
- It might be a long-standing medical thing: Your body might delay puberty if it's too busy fighting off an illness, especially if it's an ongoing one like diabetes or even asthma. If that's the case, your doctor is probably all over

it already. If you've been sick a lot but you're not getting treated yet, get your ass to the doctor double quick!

- It might be a nutritional thing: Eating nothing but crap, or not eating enough of anything, can also delay puberty. You gotta eat enough nutritious food to keep your body fueled so it can work its mojo.
- It might be a Klinefelter thing: There's something called Klinefelter's syndrome that can also keep your puberty from arriving on time. It basically means you're born with an extra chromosome that tells your body to lowball the testosterone flow. But low flow don't mean no flow, and doctors can do a lot to help with this syndrome. If the doc tells you you've got this, you're already on your way to getting help.

The good news is that doctors can test for and treat all this stuff. So, if you want to learn more, TALK TO YOUR DOCTOR!

SIZES

Andrew Coimbra

Here's the thing: a lot of us guys can get a little jealous of our home boys, not just 'cause one can shoot hoops better or 'cause the other one can draw like a madman, but because of penis size—you know, locker-room envy.

The average length of an erect penis on a fully grown guy is somewhere between 10 cm (4 inches) and 20 cm (8 inches). However, some may be smaller and some may be larger. The fact is that everyone has his own size and that's what makes life interesting—variety is the spice of life! Basically, there's no point in going all green over penis size because for every guy who's packing, there are, like, five more with bigger penises.

Besides, just because another guy has a bigger dick than yours doesn't mean that he's got it going on in bed. You can please your partner, and feel good doing it, with any sized penis. Remember, it's not what you got, but how you use it.

If you're still jealous of other guys, then think about this: the animal kingdom is totally kicking our asses in terms of penis size. A stallion's penis can be 76 cm (30 inches) long, an elephant's penis can be 1.5 meters (5 feet) or more, and the blue whale is packing 2.4 meters (8 feet)! Wow, try and beat that. But who's got the most advanced brain? We do. So use it, guys, and don't worry about your size.

Man Up!
Erectjons.

Okay, so we all know what it's like to pitch a trouser tent. But what's up, exactly, down there? Here is some technical info to help you understand what's going on inside your little friend.

What puts the *hard* in hard-on? Blood. There are two main cylinders of sponge-like tissue inside the shaft of your penis. When extra blood flows into the empty space around the tissue, your penis swells—kind of like a garden hose when the tap is on but the nozzle is closed.

So what brings on the blood? A couple of things can cause your little guy to sit up and take notice:

- **your brain:** When you have a sexual thought, your brain sends a message down through your nervous system and your dick gets ready for action—whether you want it to or not.
- **contact:** The feeling of something physically touching your penis, like your clothes, your hand, or any other stimulating sensation can also signal your penis to stiffen up.

• **your body**: Sometimes your body sends a "get an erection" message to your penis by reflex. You know those erections you wake up with in the morning? They're usually caused by having a full bladder. But next time you complain about morning wood, think about this: during an erection, your body closes a valve between your penis and your bladder so you can't pee—so it's actually helping you wait until you can get to the john! How often does your dick keep you out of trouble?

LIMPED
The Erectile Dysfunction Junction

Sometimes your dick doesn't give up the game—it stays hard for what feels like days on end and you just want it to take a breather. I mean, at some point your gonna have to write something on the chalk board at the front of the class, and when that time comes, Mr. Happy won't be welcome. But then there are the times that Mr. Happy doesn't want to get his lazy ass up, if ya know what I mean…

It's called erectile dysfunction and it sucks. There may be a number of reasons why your dick is not up for the job, but basically sex is about mind and body. Trouble with either one can mean trouble for Mr. Happy.

MIND:
Nerves
When getting ready to have sex, especially with a new partner, you might get a little nervous, which doesn't help your game. Do what you gotta do to feel comfortable and ready.

Stress
You might be thinking about other things, be upset, or be worried about something. If your brain is occupado, it won't be sending the right message to your dick. Try talking about what's on your mind before making your move.

Negative Feelings from or about Your Partner

How you feel about your partner, and how your partner expresses feelings about you, is gonna play a big part in how your parts behave. You just might not feel as turned on by your partner if you're mad or not feeling attractive or not finding your girl or guy attractive right now.

BODY:

Fatigue

You could just be tired and THAT'S normal. Your body may want to chill even if you don't. Also, if you've had too much play (recently masturbated or came during sex already), Mr. Happy will need a rest. Give him some down time.

Medication

If you're taking any medication, then it may interfere with your play. Not cool...but check with your pharmacist to see what's up (well, *down*) and what side effects to expect from your meds.

Drug or Alcohol Abuse

Using drugs and/or alcohol can cause you to go limp.

Bottom line: limp happens. If it keeps happening, check in with your doctor. Otherwise, relax and remember that there are lots of ways to have fun with your partner that don't need you to be hard.

The Juices
Your Guide to Dick Liquid

Okay, guys have outdoor plumbing, right? The penis is basically a pipe that carries liquid out of your body. There's a little tube inside your penis called the urethra and that's where the liquids flow on their way out through the hole in the head of your dick. Here's a guide to what comes out:

PISS *(urine)*
Obviously. You've been using your penis to piss since you were born. Your kidneys filter the liquid waste in your body and dump it into your bladder. When it's full, you're in charge (hopefully) of emptying your bladder through your penis. When you have an erection, a valve closes the link between the bladder and the urethra to make way for the fun stuff.

PRE-CUM *(pre-ejaculatory fluid)*
This is the little bit of clear liquid that comes out from your penis after you get an erection but before you fully cum (ejaculate). It's made by a special gland, and basically, this stuff cleans out your plumbing. Pre-cum makes the urethra less acidic (gross, science) and that gives any sperm hanging around a better

chance of surviving. Sperm normally travels in the cum, but sometimes they hitchhike with the pre-cum. That's the problem with the "withdrawal" method (pulling out) for avoiding pregnancy. Even before you officially ejaculate, there's a chance some sperm will take a ride on the pre-cum, escape through the penis into the vagina, and get the girl pregnant. Even if precum is sperm-free, it can still carry sexually transmitted infections (STIs).

CUM *(semen)*

Cum, or semen, is the milky, sticky fluid that comes out of the top of the penis when you, well, cum (ejaculate). You normally squirt out about a teaspoonful of the stuff (more if it's been a while, less if you've been busy) and it contains millions of sperm. The sperm travels from your balls and mixes with the rest of the stuff in semen, which comes from your prostate gland. The semen is then like a luxury express bus for the sperm headed to pregnancy-ville or STI city. So condom up, bro, and cut their trip short.

So Fresh and
So Clean, Clean
Hygiene Hijinks

How to make sure your penis lasts as long as you do!

The obvious thing would be to make sure that you, yourself, are clean. Shower at least every other day—every day is preferable. This includes washing your genitalia (your penis, balls, and whatever else you may have down there...), and if you are uncircumcised, make sure you pull back the hood to wash it up and rinse down.

Other stuff that you could do to make sure that you are in tip-top shape:

- **Don't smoke**—Smoking can narrow the blood vessels of your body, which can cause erectile dysfunction. Not cool. It can also lead to bladder cancer (don't worry, we didn't know that either)—not to mention lung cancer. Again, not cool.

- **Eat healthy foods**—Don't eat junky or processed foods. Less red meat is best—instead of red meat, you could eat fish or white poultry meat. Always eat lots of fresh vegetables and fruit.
- **Do something active**—Don't just sit around. Who do you think you are?! Get up. Go out with friends, exercise, take a jog, dance, join a sports team. It helps you get in shape and attract all the ladies (or guys)—everyone knows that no one can resist a sexy jock.
- **Do something relaxing**—Worrying is stressful and no one likes stress—*no* one. So make time to do stuff that chills you out. Now, don't stop taking things seriously, just make sure that crappiness doesn't consume your life. All the stuff above can help you feel better and worry less.

Being a guy and going through puberty and becoming sexual active is complicated enough. Why not make things easier by being as healthy as possible at all times? It helps to make annual check-ups with your family doctor. If you're having sex, then see the doc every six months and get tested for any STIs you might have picked up along the way.

You need to make sure that your penis is happy—so that you can be happy and ready to make your partner happy. Remember—no scrub-a-dub-dub means you gets no love. So clean up, Sucka!

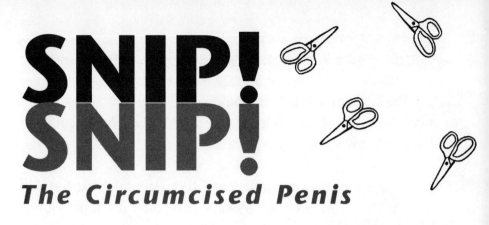

SNIP! SNIP!

The Circumcised Penis

Myke Anderson

Every guy is born with a foreskin—a flap o' skin that covers the head of his penis. Some parents have that flap cut off their baby boy. Some parents leave it there. Say hello (or goodbye) to circumcision.

Most doctors (like the American Academy of Pediatrics and the Canadian Paediatric Society) agree that circumcision is not usually medically necessary; in fact, complications from infection or screwed-up anesthetics can actually cause harm. But not everybody agrees on which is better: cut or uncut. Some people say cut (circumcised) dicks are better for STI prevention, but an uncut guy who cleans his dick properly is just as safe. Some people think uncut guys get more pleasure from sex, but that depends more on the person and the foreskin. Other people feel that getting cut is an important religious ritual. (Interesting fact: in the 1890s circumcision was thought by some people to prevent masturbation. Trust me, it doesn't work—thank God!)

The bottom line is that whether you're a v-neck or a turtle-neck, you need to live with it and KEEP IT CLEAN. Uncut guys have to know some extra tricks:

1. Uncut guys need to wash under the foreskin as well as washing the dick itself. It sounds painful but it's not (some people get off on it). Just soap up, scrub, and rinse in the shower and you should be good.

2. Uncut guys especially need to rinse their dick before they go into extra innings with their partner. Cum can get caught under the foreskin and lead to infection, which won't happen if you just wipe it off. Also, be sure to pull that foreskin back when putting on a condom.

Whatever the reason your parents decided to keep it or cut it, all dicks work just the same. So guys, just stay fresh and clean and enjoy what you got!

Balls!

Balls. Nuts. Bollocks. Cojones. Whatever you call 'em, if you've got a dick, you've also got testicles. You can't have the wiener without the beans, right? But just what are these things?

THE EQUIPMENT

Testicles

Testicles are actually internal organs, not the kind you play during the free-skate at the indoor ice rink (or maybe you do play with yours at the skating rink, but we're not here to judge), but the kind that's inside your body taking care of business. In this case, your balls' business is making testosterone and sperm, and that's what they do all day long.

Sperm-making works best when things are not too hot and not too cold. That's why your balls hang outside your body—it's too hot up in there, bro! But if it gets too cold to dangle, they'll huddle up like it's a time out at the Super Bowl. And now you know why it hurts like hell to get nailed in the nuts—they're basically internal organs on the outside. It also really hurts to get kicked in the heart, but at least that sucker is protected by your rib cage!

Scrotum

But obviously your balls aren't really hanging out all exposed. For no extra cost they come with a handsome carrying case: the scrotum. *Scrotum* is just a fancier word for "ball sack" and one size fits all. Actually, scrotums come in lots of sizes, just like testicles. Do your balls hang low? Can you toss 'em to and fro? Doesn't matter. Low or high, big or small, hanging crooked or even-steven, testicles all work the same way—unless they don't...

MALFUNCTIONS

Just like with any body part, stuff can go wrong with your balls. Since this particular body part is near and dear to most guys, it's good to know about the wrong so you can make it right again ASAP. Lucky for you, we did the legwork (ballwork?) about testicular malfunctions. Here's what we found:

Testicular Cancer

Any kind of cancer sucks balls. Testicular cancer sucks *for* your balls...and it can occur in guys as young as 15. In a nutshell (so to speak), testicular cancer is when out-of-control cancer cells start growing like mad on and around your testicles. If they grow enough, they'll start interfering with how your balls work, and can even spread to—and shut down—other parts of your body until it kills you. Shit.

The good news is that testicular cancer is completely curable IF IT IS DETECTED EARLY ENOUGH! How do you detect it? By using your fingers to cop a feel of your own balls. Squeeze 'em. Rub 'em. Get to know 'em reeeeal well, 'cause then you'll know if anything feels wrong. Wrong will feel like lumps of tissue that weren't there before. If you feel a lump, even if you THINK you feel a lump, get it checked out by your doctor. Better be safe than dead. Try to check your balls like this at least once a month, but do it behind closed doors (we're looking at you, guy-who-plays-with-his-balls-at-the-skating-rink).

Varicoceles

Very-what-now? Inside your nut sack, there are a bunch of veins bringing blood to your balls so they can do their job. A varicocele is when some valve controlling the blood flow stops doing *its* job properly and the veins have to carry an extra load. The vein gets wider and your scrotum can end up feeling like a bag of ropes. It doesn't usually hurt, but it can affect the size of your testicles and may screw things up if you want to have kids someday. It can be fixed with a simple surgery. You are most at risk of developing varicoceles between the ages of 15 and 25, but it only develops in about 1 in 6 guys.

Testicular Torsion

Erk—just the name of this one sounds painful. Testicular torsion is when one of your balls gets twisted on the cord that connects it to the inside of your body. The twisting cuts off the blood flow and it hurts like hell. That's actually a good thing because it'll make you seek help right away. Getting treatment fast is important to saving the testicle. Sometimes a doctor can fix it by carefully untwisting things by hand, but you'll still need surgery to make sure it doesn't happen again. This one is also most common in younger guys and affects 1 in 10 people.

Undescended Testicle

If you have this, doctors would probably have spotted it already 'cause you hadn't even been born yet when it happened. Or didn't happen, actually. An undescended testicle is exactly what it sounds like—when your body was forming, one of your balls didn't make the trip from being tucked up inside your body to hanging out in your scrotum. That can screw up your chances of someday having kids, so doctors would have surgically removed the undescended testicle when you were one or two years old. Sometimes, although very rarely, a kid with a hide-and-seek ball slips through to puberty without it being diagnosed. That can put a fella at a higher risk of infertility and testicular cancer. Fortunately, you can have the surgery at any age. Unfortunately, having an undescended testicle—even if it's corrected when you're a baby—puts you in a higher risk group for developing testicular cancer. So check that remaining ball for lumps as often as you can!

Epididymitis

Or what we like to call "ouchy balls." Epididymitis is actually a painful swelling of the tube connected to your balls that carries the sperm. Whatever. If your balls are red and swollen and in pain, you don't need this book to tell you to get to a doctor. We will tell you that epididymitis is often caused by sexually transmitted infections like gonorrhea and chlamydia. See Chapter 4, on STIs for more info. And for crap's sake, get to a doctor!

Blue Balls

Okay, this one isn't a malfunction. It's not even a problem compared to the other stuff on this list. Blue balls can happen if you've been turned on and hard for a long time (we're talking hours of perpetual erection) without getting off or cooling down. If this happens, your balls may ache and turn a little blue. Just like some of the veins in your arms and legs appear blue, blue balls get their color from blood with less oxygen in it. If you've been hard for hours, there's simply more blood hanging out in your crotch region. That older blood shows up blue. It may be accompanied by an uncomfortable ache, but it is NOT HARMFUL. So don't try to con your partner into thinking you'll die if you don't get off. Ain't nothing that jerking yourself off or a cold shower can't fix. Deal with it.

Wet Dreams May Come

Andrew Coimbra

A wet dream—also called a *nocturnal emission*—is when you cum (ejaculate) in your sleep. Ejaculating while you sleep is usually because you're dreaming about something sexual, but not always. The dream could be completely unrelated to sex.

Wet dreams are most common during puberty 'cause those pesky hormones are constantly telling your body to step up production of all the parts involved with sex. That means your brain gets signals to think about sex more often, your balls produce more sperm, and your penis gets hard more often. All that stuff combined can make your sleeping self get stimulated enough to release the sperm as cum (semen).

Although wet dreams are most common between the ages of 12 and 18, some guys go through puberty without ever having a wet dream, and you can still have them as an adult. Generally, wet dreams become less frequent after puberty. Also, a guy who masturbates or is otherwise regularly sexually active tends to have fewer wet dreams.

My Experience

with Wet Dreams

Anonymous

When I was 12, I started having wet dreams pretty often. I often woke up after dreaming about sex stuff and my balls would feel hot and my sheets would be wet and sticky. I felt kind of embarrassed about it whenever it happened. Some kids at school said that wet dreams were dirty and having them meant you were obsessed about sex.

Later, I started masturbating and my wet dreams stopped. It wasn't until after puberty that I realized it was very normal for teenage boys to have wet dreams during puberty. It doesn't hurt and it's not wrong; it just means that you are growing up.

I experienced it and I turned out okay, so if any kid thinks wet dreams are nasty and stuff, I would tell them that it is very normal to have them and that they happen less often when they start masturbating or when they're done puberty.

MAKING THE CONNECTION
Relationships

CHAPTER 2

Unveiled

So, you've got your family. You've got teachers. You've got friends, some from school, some from other places. You've got years of experience dealing with all kinds of people. But then along came puberty and—hello, hormones!—now you've got a whole new way of relating to people and a lot of it ain't rated G.

Okay, so not all relationships are sexual. But whether or not you're doing the deed, sex is one hell of a force that can affect how you deal with the folks around you. This chapter is mostly about those relationships where there's more going on than just friendship, but it's also about friendships where your friend is struggling with a relationship that's more than just friendship. Complicated? Yeah, well, so are relationships.

So read on to find out more about **hooking up, breaking up,** and everything in between.

KEVIN
V.

Relating

Relationship they call it, huh?

Two folks *relating* to each other, which means they *both* have a say. Relationships are like scales—if it don't balance, then it ain't right, feel me? If two peeps don't speak, there's no conversation. But don't over-exaggerate what you're saying cuz then the convo will be gonzo.

In a real relationship, men, we gotta want more than just sex. Some women think that all men are dogs barking for a piece of female flesh, but most of us really do want to interact in a way that feels right. But even if we suck at sharing our hearts, don't think it means we're not complicated. Most guys have more going on inside than they ever talk about.

Girls also have needs: sex (no shit!), communication, attention, appreciation, and most of all, RESPECT. When you look at it, girls are complicated too. They may seem more complicated than us, but they're dealing with different shit. They have their PMS, periods, and I mean they're the ones who can get pregnant, for crying out loud, so why not give them sympathy?

Problems come up in any relationship, but they're easier to deal with if you have the big two basics: trust and love.

Trust is a feeling that is earned slowly, but it can be lost quicker than money in Vegas. Sometimes problems pop up faster than Jordan hops, but if you trust each other anything can be overcome.

Love is such a strong word that it could make you get butterflies or crush you like orange soda. Never ever unleash such a word on your partner unless you feel it and the time is right. Don't get it wrong and mix up just *liking* someone with actually *loving* them. But if you do both feel it, ain't nothing better for a relationship.

Coupling!
Seven Signs of Good Lovin'

Some things we need to have in order to have a healthy relationship are not so hard for us to do. Most of these require minimal energy.

1) RESPECT:
You and your partner respect each other's choices. That makes you both feel comfortable telling about things the other might disagree with. Say if you're really in the mood and ready to hit the sack with your partner but your partner isn't into it. "Not tonight, babe." "That's OK, baby."

2) EQUALITY:
You and your partner play by the same rules. Say, it's you and your girl: you have friends who are girls, and she will have friends who are guys. You spend time alone with those friends and she spends time alone with her friends. Equality and compromising in a relationship makes life a lot more exciting...even in the bedroom! Like, if you want your partner to go down on you, you should be willing to down on your partner, too.

3) TRUST:

You and your partner each believe what the other says and you don't freak out about what the other is doing when you're apart. Most people have a hard time with this one. It's hard to trust someone when you're a rookie to the relationship game, but trusting your partner makes the relationship much more comfortable to be in and your partner easier to open up to.

4) HONESTY:

You and your partner can tell each other things even if it's difficult. What if a girl or guy that you find attractive calls you up to study with you? You should be able to tell your partner about it and your partner should respect your honesty and decision.

5) TIME ALONE:

You and your partner can spend time apart. It's good to have separate friends and activities, and it's good to realize that your lives don't revolve around each other. If you are always together, things could get a bit stale and you might feel isolated from the rest of your life, so it's important to maintain some time for yourself.

6) SUPPORT:

You and your partner are there for each other. You know your partner better than most people, and when things go down, you can provide support and understanding.

7) COMMUNICATION:

You and your partner can talk, talk, talk. Talking to each other keeps things interesting and keeps the misunderstandings at a minimum. Communication is also listening. It's always good to know who you're involved with.

Uncoupling!

Five Ways to Ruin a Relationship

Any of these things will ruin a healthy relationship:

1) MIND GAMES:

You or your partner tries to be manipulative by saying stuff that makes the other feel bad. To get what you want, one of you might say: "If you love me, you'll have sex with me." or "I love you but I'm not *in* love with you."

2) JEALOUSY:

You or your partner is very possessive and tries to control who the other spends time with. "I don't like the way that guy looks at you. You're not hanging around with him anymore."

3) Co-Dependency:

You and your partner feel like you can't get emotional support from anybody except each other. "If you don't love me, nobody will."

4) Disrespect:

You or your partner does or says things that will hurt the other—for example, name-calling or cheating. This might be behind the other person's back, in person, or in front of other people.

5) Threats or Violence:

You or your partner uses, or threatens to use, physical force against the other. This is abuse and it's *never* okay!

Commitment

Antonio Giovanni Rumere

I think I have a hard time with commitment because I get easily distracted by pretty women.

On one occasion, I remember my boys brought me to this house jam. At the time, I was going out with this sweet girl, and I didn't plan to do anything with anyone else because I didn't want to mess up what we had. But then I started drinking, and I got to know this other girl, and she got the better of me if u know what I mean.

I know that it's an unhealthy relationship if you don't show the other person any sign of respect, you don't listen, or you're always disrespecting the person you're supposed to be with. On the other hand, I find it hard to talk with a girl about what it means to be faithful.

I think that a healthy relationship needs three key factors:

1) **Communication.** If you're having a hard time communicating with the person you like, either you've got to try harder or find someone else that you can communicate with.

2) **Trust.** If you can't trust the person you like, and they can't trust you, then there is no point in both of you wasting your time.

3) **Loyalty.** If you're not loyal with your partner, why should you be upset if you're always thinking that the other person is cheating on you? 'Cause that's what happens when you cheat. You both have to decide what it means to be loyal and then do it.

I'm telling you from experience, if you do not have these three things, best believe that your person ain't calling you no more.

Love?

Antonio Giovanni Rumere

Love may come and love may go
but loving you is what I want to show
You're the most precious jewel of God's creation
A source of my thought and my inspiration
This life that I live will never last forever
but I will truly remember all the moments that
we spent together.
If there is one thing that I want to cherish
it is for my love to stay eternal
Even with all this publicity and all of this fame
The time that I spent away from you has set
us apart but deep down
inside we believe that we're attached at heart
You always think that I will forget about you
but how would it happen when everything I do
Is thinking about holding you in my arms
every day and every night because according to
my heart that's the only thing
that I feel is right
The time has come for me to say good-bye
maybe take a couple of seconds to calm myself
and cry
Not because I realized that our relationship is
dangling on a string but because I realized
that without you I'm nothing

KEVIN VUONG

Being a Man,
Flexing My Muscles...

Marlon Anderson

Come on guys, all ya'll know that some-times we as guys try to act like we're the shit. I mean, we all try to put up a front when we are around our boys, acting like we're all thugs, gangsters, playboys, etc. But on a real tip, both you and I know that it is just a mask that we put on at times to impress our friends and G's.

I can be a man and admit that there were mad times when I tried to be something I knew that I wasn't. Boy did I front. I would do things that I did not want to do because I was too interested in impressing my boys from my hood. For example, I got into many fights that I wouldn't have if my boys hadn't been there. I would also do things like bun weed, get drunk, and even have sex with certain G's that I wasn't even really feeling for just to belong to a popular crowd.

I ain't even going to front still: most of the things that I allowed my boys to influence me into doing made me into a local celebrity in my hood. Let me tell you, when I was the shit, everyone wanted to be my friend. Not to sound cocky, but I had G's and dudes begging to chill with me. I was even a part of a gang for a minute. Yo, I was on cloud nine, but all of that fame came crashing down like a wrecked plane in the end. I was shot at, and had to move away from my neighborhood for a while. Check this, I even had people approaching my house, telling my grandmother that they were looking for my ass. I then started being harassed by the police.

The turning point in my life was when I got arrested. Where were all of my so-called boys 4 life? And I ended up getting kicked out of my crib because I had decided that it would be cool to thief my granny's car with my boys when she went away on vacation. I drove home drunk and ended up totaling the car. When I was kicked out on the street, my boys, who I thought would be there 4 life, never cared about what I was going through. And no other family member of mine wanted to have nothing to do with me because everyone was just totally fed up with my behavior.

All that shit going down was a wake-up call for me. I stood up and said, Enough is enough. Fuck what my boys, other

people, and even G's had to say about me. I was ready to be a man and take full responsibility for my actions. Listen, a real man takes control of his life, and only a punk lets his boys control his every move. I can flex my muscles by taking full control of my life and doing the right things—not what others want me to do.

Ride

Anonymous, 18

Sometimes I feel like I'm being neglected
Maybe it's because of my mistakes or the shit that I reflected
From my behavior and actions full of scandals
to all my boys that you said are only low-life vandals
Crippin ain't easy, that's what Snoop said
Well life ain't easy either—I gotta get paid
Gotta wife now and a baby on the way
and I can only kneel down and pray
for better dayz so all this shit could go away
I want all the miseries to go so only the happiness will stay
Sometimes I feel like I'm losing my mind and sanity
but most days I don't feel like I can think with enough clarity
GOD I'm wondering if you hear my prayers
cuz I'm feeling that I'm sinking in deep water
If I don't see you again I hope to see you later
as I'm off to start a new chapter
in my life that's full of danger, murder, and homicide
that sometimes makes me feel that I should commit suicide
Deep down inside I'm hoping that you will ride
with me cuz I really need you by my side

JUNGLE FEVER

Marlon Anderson

Here's my story of an interracial relationship and some of the complications that came along with it. When I was just starting high school, there was this white girl in my homeroom class. She was a dime—every guy in the school wanted to get with her, but she never seemed to be interested in any of them. She and I didn't speak at first, but we started giving each other long steamy eye contact. After a couple of months, we started bumping shoulders on purpose in the hallway just to have physical contact.

Eventually, we started having small conversations with each other during class and then finally we exchanged digits. For a long time, I wanted to ask her to be my girl, but there was something bothering me deep down inside. I mean, I knew that she was a good girl and she was everything that I wanted in a girlfriend, so what was the problem? What was I waiting for? The truth is, it made me nervous that she was white and I was black. I was very intimidated to let anyone know, even her, how I felt.

Anyway, even though I wasn't sure about it, we started dating. It was all good at the beginning, but then she started getting upset at me for one particular reason. She would always say, "How come you never want to be close to me in school, but when we're just by ourselves, you are all over me?" and I would always say, "Because a lot of guys like you and I don't want them to try to fuck with our relationship, so let's keep it low." But she was never pleased with the way we kept our relationship so silent. She wanted to hold hands in the halls and make out in the cafeteria. That's not what I wanted because of that one fear that had been holding me captive from the start.

One day, one of my boys found out about me and my secret love affair, and of course, he ran around the school and let everyone know. I guess that's where the saying comes in: "What's done in the dark shall come to light." Well that day everything sure did come to light, a very bright one. Walking down the hall in my school, I seen a huge group of my boys and girls standing there, waiting for me, like an army ready for war. As I approached the group to see what all the excitement was about, the fear that haunted me for months hit me right in the face. They started singing "JUNGLE FEVER! YOU GOT JUNGLE FEVER!"

My secret was out. My schoolmates, who I thought were my friends, started clowning on the fact that I had been dating a white girl. And not only did my boys rag on me, but my father, who found out from my big-mouth brother, made me feel so low and worthless. My father, who I thought was supposed to be there for me as a role model and friend, told me very clearly that he did not want me talking to white girls and that I better tell her to move on because she will not be accepted into our family. He said that white girls are trouble and that they only want black men because they have big dicks.

So, I gave in to my father and to my concerns about my popularity at school, and I told the girl that I didn't want to see her anymore. We never spoke to each other again. We would see each other in the halls and pass each other as if it was just two total strangers on the street. But even though that situation had happened, I never did stop thinking of her.

MEET *the* *Parents*

Kenny Vuong

The first time I had to meet my girlfriend's parents was when I went to pick her up to go to the movies. They just asked me what we were doing and where we were going. I said we were just on our way to see a movie about snakes on a plane. Then we left to go to the mall, and I remembered it was her birthday, too. So I made sure I had money so I could buy her that new jacket she wanted.

After the movie, we were hungry. We bought lunch at the mall's food court and we saw her parents and started to talk again. Then I had to go to the washroom. While I was in the washroom, my girlfriend said her parents were talking about what a gentleman I am and how courteous I am. When I came out of the washroom, my girlfriend had to go to the washroom, so I was left sitting alone with my girlfriend's parents. I had this weird feeling like I had butterflies in my stomach. Then I felt really scared because I thought I wasn't answering their questions correctly. So then my girlfriend's parents left and I was left waiting for her.

When she came out, we started to walk out of the mall. We got near the exit and then I remembered that jacket. I told her to hold on for just a second. As she waited for me, I bought her that jacket she had wanted for the past four months. When I showed her the jacket, her reaction was priceless. It was like looking at the sunset and the sunrise at the same time. So she gave me a kiss, and I gave one back.

As we walked home, she asked me what me and her parents talked about when she was in the washroom. I said, "Oh, we were just talking about how good a boyfriend I am to you and stuff like that." She said, "Oh, okay." Before she left, I said, "Wait a minute. I need to give you something." She said, "What?" Then I gave her a kiss that was about one minute long and I said, "Happy Birthday," and she went home. Then I went to play basketball.

Black Diamond

Antonio Giovanni Rumere

I know I'm not the best-looking guy out there
but you have to know I will always care
Every time I see your beautiful face
my body shivers and my heart increases pace
I love you just the way you are
If I can't love you near I'll love you from afar
2 is not a number, a point, or a score
It means us together though I fear there will be more
I'll run to the end of the world
just to show my feelings for you
I'll do every single thing that you want me to do
Time passes but my feelings keep on climbing
because you're a Black Diamond that can't stop shining
I always think that I am so lucky
to have you standing right beside me
Baby girl I hope you can understand and you can see
That my life without you would be nothing but empty.

Plenty of Fish in the Sea...
STRAIGHT Fish!

Andrew Coimbra

You know the old saying. People will always tell you after you break up with someone that "there are plenty of other fish in the sea." Well, I'm here to tell you that it may be true, but few of those fish are full-blown angelfish—if ya know what I mean. And that can make it difficult to find another fish to love!

I'm talking about us non-straight guys out there. If you think it's a challenge for a straight guy to find a girl he cares about, it's *really* difficult for gay and bisexual guys to even meet other gay/bi

guys our own age. It really is. I mean, it's kind of depressing not being able to find someone your age to hang out with, let alone share the world with. Cheesy, but love is, isn't it?

The worst part is, when you finally do meet someone, you might be tempted to stay with him even if the guy is no good for you. Basically, don't be foolish. You're gay. Gay people are smart. I mean, I am (don't hate, appreciate). Just remember, sooner or later the right guy will come along and you'll be happy. Crazy happy! So good luck, and don't be too quick to make decisions.

Being Me and Gay

Nick, 17

I used to think being gay was going to make my life really hard. I was afraid to tell my mom and my friends. I thought I would get made fun of and people would hate me. I thought this when I was 12. Now I am 17, and I think being gay has made me a better person. Now, I don't mean I am better than straight people. I mean that I am a stronger, more confident person. And because of that, I have great friends, and I am more involved in my school. When I was 12, I thought my world was over, but it wasn't—it was just beginning.

I know what you are thinking. You think, how can being gay be the best thing that ever happened to you? Well, it isn't about being gay; it's about being me and gay and about learning who I am and how I can fit into this world. It's about learning who really matters to me. It's about learning to stand up for myself and about being proud. Being gay has helped me learn those things. I am me... strong, confident, loyal, and gay.

Now, that's not to say that everything is perfect. Some of the guys in my school think it's funny to call me names. But the best thing about being confident is that the name-calling doesn't make me feel bad about myself. It makes me feel bad about them and sometimes it makes me angry, but they can't hurt me. They can't take away my mom, my friends, or my confidence. I know who I am—do they?

Me and my friends started a Gay-Straight Alliance in our school. We have a great teacher who helps out, and the vice-principal told me she thinks our group is just what the school needs. I belong in this school. I have a place and purpose. Once I felt that school was too much and that I didn't fit in. Now I know I can not only go to school but also be a part of it. The best part is that now I know that there are other gay kids in my school. If there are more of us who are confident and proud of who we are, then maybe the bullies who still think it's funny to make fun of us will lose interest.

I know when I leave high school, I will have my mom, my friends, good grades, and my Gay-Straight Alliance experiences to help me go to university or college, or travel around the world, or do anything I want to do. Being gay isn't going to stop me from reaching my dreams. I am going to do all the things I want to do, **and being gay has taught me that it is all** possible.

THE WRITING ON THE WALL
MY EXPERIENCE WITH
Homophobia

Curtis Winter

When I was 16 years old, I knew I was gay but I wasn't out yet. One day near the end of grade 10, I was coming home from school when I saw it. I was walking along the path that leads to the front of my building when I noticed something had been painted in huge letters on the wall: *CJ IS A FAG*. CJ was my nickname.

I just stopped and stared at it for a while. I wanted to cry. I was very ashamed and hurt that someone hated me so much they would do that to me at the place I lived. I didn't know what to do, so I just ran inside to my room.

Then my mom came home with my sister and step-dad. They had all seen it. My mom tried to be sensitive to my feelings and talk to me about, but I didn't want to. Instead, I just grabbed a bucket of paint from under the sink and painted over that writing again and again till it was gone.

I never found out who did it. Since then, I've come out, and it has sometimes been hard, but you know what? That writing on the wall was probably still the meanest thing anyone has ever done to me in my entire life.

Dusky Boy

Anonymous, 18

Calm down pretty boy
Playing it cool and easy
Letting your eyelids droop lazily
Making my inside burn at the thought of you ignoring me
But then your matted hair frizzles and gives you away
I could never run my fingers through those dreaded locks
But I know you'd give me time to untangle every single strand
If I wanted
Calm down little boy
Spreading out your darkly clothed legs
Leaning down like a man into comfortable silence
Making my cheeks burn red as I gripped the pole to steady
   my mind
Feeling me pass you as the train shudders to a halt,
As I shiver and release
I walk off the car, doors closing
I look back and stare into your eyes, and you stare back
   into mine

The train picks up speed, yet we still keep this gaze unbroken,
Until finally you are gone, into complete darkness
And I am left standing in a deserted subway station
At one in the morning,
Thinking how I'll never see you again
Calm down, dusky boy
Sitting only five seats away from me
On an empty subway car
Making my palms sweat with a glance at your smooth skin
Metal rings and bars interrupting the gentle line of your nose
In my mind my fingers run over each pierced crevice
Tracing over the cold, steel scars
Fondling their perfection

The BIG Conversation
Coming Out to Parents

Andrew Coimbra

During our sexual lifetimes, there are some conversations we never want have to have with our parents. But, hey, some topics are unavoidable. Ever had to tell your parents something like "I got someone pregnant" or "I have a sexually transmitted infection"? If yes, then you know it can be scary as hell. Well, for many gay people, telling their parents they are gay is one of the scariest things they will ever have to do. Let's face it, being young and lesbian, gay, or bisexual means you have to put up with a lot. Some people think all kinds of negative things about gay people *and* all kinds of negative things about teenagers, so being both can cause you a lot of problems.

If you are gay, you know what I'm talking about. But hey, you've made it this far, right? It sucks to have to hide who you are from the people around you. It's exhausting and it can make you pull away from the people that are close to you, including your parents. If you decide that you do want to tell them you are gay, you're gonna want to prepare. Make a plan, man.

Here are some ideas:

Do it when you feel ready

Coming out is a huge decision and it's something you should only do when you are ready. Don't come out to your parents because someone else is pressuring you to do it. Make sure it is *your* decision. And whatever you do, don't come out to your parents when you are drunk, high, or angry. That's just asking for trouble. Don't sweat it if you keep changing your mind about when you're gonna do it. Sometimes it just isn't the right time. The good news is that you have plenty of time, so don't rush into anything.

Pick a time and place

You're in charge, so plan the event carefully. Pick a time and place that makes you feel safe and in control. Also pick a time when you and your folks can actually talk. Don't do it right before they have to go to work or when your grandma is on her way over with a pork roast. Pick somewhere that is comfortable for you and private. You want someplace familiar, like your living room, but you don't want your little brother bursting in with his friends.

Be prepared

You know all about being a real-life gay person, right? But your parents might not have a lot of real information about gay people. Fire up your printer, brush off your library card, and gather some FAQ sheets, articles, books, or pamphlets to help them learn more. If you look around (like on the websites listed in Resources, starting on page 225), you'll find that there is some great information available for parents. There are even other parents out there who can help folks like yours understand and support their gay kids.

Have a safety plan

Like with a fire drill, you want to know where to go and what to do in an emergency. Truth is, no matter how well you plan all this, sometimes things don't go down the way we want them to. Make sure you have somewhere safe to go to if your parents react badly. Maybe a friend's house. Your parent's may just need some time to cool off, but don't get caught by surprise. You don't want to suddenly have nowhere to go or no one to turn to.

Be patient

You've probably known you were gay for a long time. Your folks, on the other hand, are likely hearing it (or even thinking about it) for the first time. Don't be surprised if they need some time to think about it and accept it. Remember that they may know nothing about gay people except a bunch of myths. But stay cool, be patient, and let them learn more. Help them when they need it.

Be direct and honest

Take a deep breath and just tell them you are gay. Seriously, it's usually easier to just come out and say it. Talking around it and avoiding using the g-word can just make everybody more nervous and cause a lot of confusion. Let your folks know you love them and tell them what you need from them. Even if they can't or won't give it to you right away, it's important that you say it. Answer any questions they have as honestly and clearly as you can. Yeah, it may be uncomfortable for all of you, but honesty can help build that trust stuff, and you're going to need a lot of both to get through this.

Reflect

Okay, after you've told your parents and when you are alone, take a deep breath and relax. Coming out to parents is one of the most difficult things a gay person can do and you have just done it! So maybe it didn't go the way you hoped, wrapped up all neat and tidy like some 1980s sitcom, but it's done and you rock for doing it. Think about what you just accomplished and be proud of yourself, bro!

Let's face it, coming out to parents is never gonna be an easy thing to do. It's risky business—some people lose their families when they come out. So think about your family and how they might react. Some parents are accepting right away and some may take years to be cool with it. Either way, make sure you have your own support system of people such as friends, teachers, and/or counselors to help you out. Remember, too, that there is plenty of support available to parents and families. PFLAG (Parents, Families and Friends of Lesbians and Gays) is an organization that helps parents deal with the news that their child is gay. Check out the back of this book for more info about PFLAG and other organizations like it.

TREAD SOFTLY WHAT TO DO WHEN YOUR FRIEND Comes Out

Andrew Coimbra

What do you do if you are straight and you have a friend who tells you that he is gay? You might feel weird at first. After all, we often hear a lot of negative stuff about gay people, right? But remember that he is your friend. He was gay before he told you, even if you didn't realize it. He hasn't changed, but his telling you might change the way you think about him.

Instead of freaking out, take some time to think about why you may feel uncomfortable. Just because your friend is gay, it doesn't mean he wants to suck your dick. More likely, he just wants you to keep being his friend no matter what. The most important thing you can do is support him. So tread softly and assure him that you are still his friend and that you won't tell anyone that he's gay. This is his information, so let him tell people when he's ready. Coming out can be a really hard thing to do. You can make it easier. Here are some tips:

Don't panic

There is a lot of misinformed shit out there about gay people. If we don't know anyone who is gay, it can be hard to know what to expect. We might get nervous, uncomfortable, or even a little spooked. Just remember that this is your friend. You know him. Plus, there is lots of solid, honest info available about gay people. Take some time to find it and learn more.

Don't question him

When someone comes out, a lot of times our first reaction is to ask "Are you sure?" Think about how hard it must be to tell someone that you are gay. Most people are damn sure before they say it out loud to someone. Remember, you may be hearing this for the first time, but your friend has been thinking about it for a loooooooong time.

Tell him you are his friend

One of the scariest things about coming out is the fear of losing the people you love and rely on. Well, friends rely on each other—especially during hard times. So let your friend know you will be there for him, from womb to tomb, from birth to earth. Even if you're uncomfortable at first, let him know you are still his friend. You have plenty of time to relax about it and learn more about gay people.

Don't tell anyone

Coming out is way personal. Gay people need to do it when they are ready and with the people they choose. No one should do it for them. You wouldn't want someone blabbing your personal secrets all over, would you? If a friend tells you that he is gay, it means he trusts you. Don't break that trust by telling other people. Your friend might be coming out only to you now, or to you and his family, so don't assume he wants his info made public; it's his coming out and his schedule.

Support him

When your friend begins to tell more people, things could get dicey. Some of his friends might reject him, or maybe his parents will not be so supportive. Other people may start to harass him and call him names. Let him know you still support him.

Learn more

If you don't know a lot about gay people, find out more. There is a lot of bullshit out there, so be careful where you look. Check out the Resources at the back of this book for some websites, or ask your friend where you can get more information.

Tomboys *and* Pussies

Against Gender Norms

Myke Anderson

What makes you a guy? I mean, mentally. Sure, you have a dick, you don't have a vagina (right?), and all that stuff. But I want to know, inside your head, what makes you a guy?

Think about it: when you were born, you didn't know anything about what it meant to be a guy. You were just a baby. You didn't even know what a penis was, so it sure didn't matter what size it was. You didn't know that you were supposed to like girls and cars and hockey... that was all just stuff. No meaning. Just stuff. So how do you go from being a baby, with no beliefs, to having certain ideas about being a man, a real man?

We're taught since we're babies about which ideas are expected to go with each gender, so we don't have a lot of control over it. Some parents "help" a lot—"Don't cry! Be a big boy," or "Dolls are for girls," and stuff like that. But it's also in pictures, in books, and on TV. Think of a police officer. Who do you see? Probably a man. Think of a nurse. You see a woman, right? Why? Aren't there female cops and male nurses? We immediately think of one gender as the "right" gender for that job. We often use these kinds of gender ideas to define somebody else without knowing anything else about them.

We define other people this way, but we also define ourselves. And what happens when those definitions we've been taught don't fit? What about a boy who doesn't like cars or sports? He gets shit for it. Pansy, pussy, woman, queer, fag.... What about a girl who doesn't care about dresses or pink? She gets called dyke, frigid, or tomboy. What about transgendered people? They get harassed more than anyone. We need to ask ourselves why are people who don't fit stereotypical definitions punished for it?

Like I said earlier, think about it. There are lots of people who don't fit into the neat little boxes of what a "man" should be, so stop labeling people because they don't act masculine or feminine enough for you. It's unfair, it's wrong, and you're only showing how stupid you are when you do it.

TRAPPED

Jordan Cleveland, 15

Trapped in a cage of flesh
Feeling so incomplete
Thinking about his future
And the girl he will never be

Mentally he is a woman
Physically he is a boy
His emotions rip him apart
And he feels tossed aside
   like a toy

His classmates cast him stares
Looks of disgust and hate
He has hidden her for so long
But this girl cannot simply wait

She is clawing at the bars
She wants her chance to
   finally shine
And the boy sits in the corner
Wondering if this flaw is
   by design

He ponders this for some time
He sees that it is not a flaw
Him is her and he is she
And he will not let her fall

He has fought it many years
And he knows the hurt is
   strong
Today he may be a boy
Today, but not for long.

PAPER CUT
Thoughts on Jealous Fellas

Lucas Perez

"Beware of jealousy!" says Shakespeare. "It is the green-eyed monster which doth mock the meat it feeds on." Whatever that means.

Personally, I think of jealousy as that possessive feeling you get when you really want to be with someone, but you think (or know) that that person is interested in somebody else. I admit that I've felt jealous before and it led me to act like a complete asshole. One time, a guy I know kissed a girl that I wanted to kiss and I got so pissed at him, even though she wasn't even my girlfriend. Another time, when I did have a girlfriend, I thought she was being too flirty with another guy and I got pissed at her. Both times I got mad over nothing, and I apologized for my actions.

Sometimes people in a relationship can't help feeling jealous. If they can talk about it and deal with it, though, it is completely normal and healthy. Jealousy becomes unhealthy if it ends up being the root of every conflict. In some cases, jealousy can lead to abusive behavior, where one person tries to control the other by using manipulation, threats, or even violence. If you think that your jealousy is like this or you know of someone who is like this, check out the back of this book for places where you can find help.

Jealousy is something that you need to control— not something that should control you.

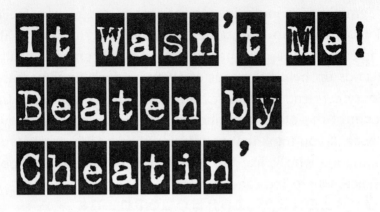

It Wasn't Me! Beaten by Cheatin'

Anonymous

Hey, I don't want to give a bad rep to us guys here, but the fact is some of us cheat on our partners. Does any of this sound familiar?

"I was thinking about you the whole time!" (yeah, right)

"I had too much to drink!"

"It was just a fling but truly you're the one that I want to be with."

"I promise I won't do it again."

I don't care how you define *cheating*, whether it's kissing somebody else or screwing somebody else, we know it when we're doing it. I want to talk about why some of us do it. I think there are a few reasons:

1. We're afraid of a long-lasting commitment.
2. We've had a bad experience at home, like if one of our parents cheated on the other, and it's messed up how we roll in our own relationships.

3. We just don't have the balls to break up a relationship that we don't want to be in anymore.

It's that last one that pisses me off the most. Guys, if we don't want to be with someone, we got to pony up and do the right thing. Before you screw around with somebody else, gather all your strength and tell your current partner straight up that the relationship is over.

And yeah, I know, there are plenty of girls who cheat, too. Whether you're the victim or the perpetrator, the point is that cheating sucks. Like the old saying says, "Treat others as you'd like to be treated." If you respect someone's feelings right now, chances are better that, in the future, someone else is going to respect yours.

Jacob Blomme

FIGHTING
Deal with It

In a relationship, fights happen. My girlfriend and I don't get along all the time. It can be really annoying if an argument happens over and over and you get nowhere with it. But fighting can be a good thing, too.

My experience with fighting is that it's all about airing out your shit and giving each person a chance to listen. I think conflict can be positive 'cause I'd rather argue about something than have someone bottle up what's bothering them until they blow up about a situation.

I know most of you guys have heard the phrase "I'm fine" from your girlfriend, when you know that, in fact, she's pissed at you but she doesn't want to talk about it. The trick is to get her to vent it so she can let it go. If she can say what's wrong, then it's out in the open and you can talk about it. You usually can't

and Move On

solve the problem right away—most times it takes more arguing before you find a solution. Make sure you listen to her and hear what she's saying, or else she's going to be mad for a while and that's not good for anyone.

Another tip is don't assume that you did something wrong 'cause lots of the time, when my girlfriend is mad, it has been at someone else or something else. Then you can ask, "Is there anything I can do?" My experience is that she will say "No," but at least she can see that you're trying so she's got to cut you a bit of slack.

My advice on arguing is don't run from it *but* don't get fully caught up in it either. If you can catch it early, it will be easier to resolve and you can both move on and get back to having a good time.

Not So Small Talk about Relationships

Cris, 17

For me, the most important things in a relationship are patience and respect. Maybe most people would say things like loyalty, trust, or love, but I think all of those go out the window if you don't have patience or respect.

The thing is, in any relationship, your partner is going to do things that annoy you. You have to learn to stay calm and look past the annoying things because they aren't worth fighting about. There will be bigger things that you're gonna have to deal with, but you have to know how to do it respectfully.

The biggest thing I ever had to deal with happened two years ago. My girlfriend missed her period so I thought I was going to be a father. I was only 15 and we had only been going out for a year so I was confused and angry and almost every emotion you can go through. I told my girlfriend we should do a pregnancy test. She took the test and it came out negative, but I didn't trust it so I took her to a clinic and we got the same results. After this incident, we started being more careful.

That's when I really learned that it's not worth getting upset over small things. Patience and respect. If you don't have these things, your relationship will fall apart because then you'll be fighting all the time. If you can't get along over little stuff, how are you gonna be over the big stuff?

Forever Friend

Lucas Perez

A shoulder to cry on, a listening ear
Attraction to a friend now trying to think clear
Guys came and went, all I did was watch
I didn't say a word 'cause in my throat my heart was caught
Never too close, at a distance I stood my place
As I fought the temptation to touch and caress your face
My feelings for you, I can't share
'cause of reactions I don't care to dare
Wondered what would happen if I stole a kiss
Would you reject it or would I taste your lips
I want the best for you, see you happy, and
see you smile
Even if it hurts me and keeps me in denial
Oblivious to what I feel, you crush it time and time again
Each and every time you tell me we're just friends.
But I understand
Our friendships is too precious to play
With that done and said
I'll forever be your friend even through sunny and cloudy days.

GIVE ME A BREAK
The Dumper and the Dumped

Breaking up. Sooner or later we all go through it. If you've been dumped, you know that it feels all kinds of crappy. But sometimes you gotta be the dumper. How do you know if you're ready to go? Some stuff to think about:

- Make one of those pro and con lists. Cheesy, but it works.
- Figure out what's changed between you. Is it something you can fix? Is it something you even want to fix?
- Talk to someone who's spent a good amount of time on the relationship train. Perspective is key, bro.

If you decide getting out is what you gotta do, how do you do it? Here are some ideas on how to break up... without The Dumped wanting to break your face:

- The most important thing is to end it by telling your partner straight up how you feel.
- Don't be an asshole about it. Don't play the blame game and don't start name-calling.
- Face to face is best, and do it somewhere quiet—without your or her or his friends around.
- Keep it short. You don't have to have a big ol' conversation about your deepest feelings. Just be clear that you've made your decision and stick to it.

Remember, there is no point continuing the relationship anymore if one of you isn't interested.

EX FACTOR
Dealing with a Former Flame

Antonio Giovanni Rumere

Have you ever felt that your ex is bothering you or your new partner? What should you do when your ex can't let you go?

TIPS
1. Be honest. Tell your ex straight up that the relationship is over.
2. Set ground rules. Make it clear what kind of behavior is NOT okay, like calling you constantly, calling your new flame, or coming to your house uninvited.
3. Stay calm. Don't go crazy and start yelling. You want to be able to solve problems with calmness, so that you don't start new issues or rehash old ones.

If your ex keeps on coming up to you, then you may have to get help from your friends and family. Let them know that your ex isn't respecting your ground rules. Having others support those rules might help your ex realize that you really mean it. However, some people have a really hard time moving on. If things continue or get worse, talk to a school counselor or nurse or contact one of the organizations at the back of this book. You're dealing with harassment and you're gonna need heavy backup.

Whatever the outcome, it's important that you've tried to solve the problem without losing your temper. You should give props to yourself for this, because no one else did it but you.

Let You Flow

Jacob Blomme

I see you hiding in my eyes
I tell you I'm fine but that's a lie
I want to try ... push these feelings outside
Why can't I cry... I feel lonely inside...

How long can I hold you until I react
The pressure's so strong it's pushing me back
I feel stuck in this emotional trap

You disappear once I have smoked
This lump in my throat makes me choke
Continue to smoke so you don't provoke

Why are you a part of me? And why won't you go away?
I try to hide you hoping that you'll come another day
But you make it clear to me that you're here to stay

I feel like I hate you and everything you bring
I can't think, sleep, or focus on a thing

You sit inside me until I can let you go
No one's around, I'm all alone
So let's go...
Let these fucking tears flow

Tough "LOVE"?
Violence and Relationships

You know how in school, when there's a scrap, people stand around watching it chanting, "FIGHT! FIGHT!"? Then the teachers roll up and grab the people fighting—and even some of the spectators. And then when authorities are handing out punishments, those spectators will all be saying, "I didn't do anything!" Exactly.

Now what if, instead of two guys whaling on each other behind the gym, you have a friend who is abusing his partner and you know about it? Not doing anything about that is even worse.

The problem is that you may feel it's not your business. However, it's your obligation as a friend to do something. If you really are friends with the guy but won't say anything, who will? You need to get your shit together and tell your friend EVERYTHING that's on your mind. Here's some stuff to know going in:

- Let him know that you're still his friend, but what he's doing is wrong and it's got to stop.
- Don't let him get away with excuses. Abuse is never okay.
- Try to convince him to talk to someone about it. See the Resources in the back of this book for info on who to call.
- Don't get stuck being the middleman between him and his partner. You're his friend, dammit, not a marriage counselor.

No matter how it goes down, you should also talk about all this to an adult you trust. This is some serious shit and you'll want the backup.

HEALTHY *Relationship*

Q & A

Interview by the Group

Courtnay McFarland, Manager of Youth Services, Davenport Perth Neighborhood Centre in Toronto (www.dpnc.ca) interviewed by the Group

Q: What makes a healthy relationship?

A: A healthy relationship is based on equality. Both partners should feel that they exercise equal and balanced power and control. Some other characteristics of a healthy relationship include: trust, mutual support, having a good connection with other people, good communication (including openness to negotiation), and feeling good and safe emotionally, physically, and sexually.

Q: What do you do if you are not in a healthy relationship?

A: If at any point you feel that your relationship has more bad characteristics than good ones, then you need to think carefully about whether or not you want to be in that relationship. You should talk to other people that you trust and respect. Their perspectives and experiences may help you to sort out your options if you decide to end a bad relationship.

Q: Do you think arguments are healthy in a relationship?

A: I think a healthy relationship needs arguments. Arguments are not a problem if you can find a solution that both partners agree on. Arguments become a problem if one partner gives in just to please the other or if the issue is left unresolved in some other way.

Q: Do you think that someone's experience in past relationships is beneficial to a present relationship?

A: Relationships should always be about learning. Each relationship helps you get to know yourself, how you are at communicating in different situations, what you need to feel happy and safe, and how to develop the skills that make a relationship work. Of course, you also learn from your mistakes. When you step into a relationship, you try to not make the same mistakes that you made in the past while encouraging what has worked successfully for you before.

Q: Do you think an age difference matters when it comes to relationships?

A: Age does not necessarily tell us anything about a person's maturity level. You could be 17 years old but have the maturity level of a 20 year old, and vice versa. Most important is that a relationship has a strong level of equality and mutual respect between both partners. When one partner is considerably younger, however, there is more often a concern that the relationship is not equal. It is important to question, for example, why an 18-year-old would want to have a 13-year-old partner. Is the relationship equal or is one partner more powerful and taking advantage of the other?

Q: Why do you think that some people cheat on their partners?

A: Sometimes, I think there are as many reasons for people behaving in certain ways as there are people. Even so, in working with youth, I've seen some reasons come up pretty often. I think sometimes people are afraid to end a relationship, so they step into another relationship without properly breaking off the old one. Other people cheat because they are angry at their partner or because they like the thrill of doing something forbidden. Still other people simply give in to temptation if someone other than their partner expresses an interest. The important thing to understand is that, whether your intentions are fair or not, you will have a profound effect on your partner if you decide to cheat. Be responsible.

Q: How do you know if a person isn't giving consent to sex?

A: Words or body language should express how the person is feeling. If at any point you can't tell whether or not your partner consents, you need to ask. Ideally, people should be talking about sex long before having it—not just when they are naked and in bed but also when they are fully clothed and relaxed. Clear communication outside the bedroom helps ensure clear communication in the bedroom.

Q: What are the different types of abuse in relationships that people should watch out for?

A: There are many forms that abuse can take. **Physical abuse** is most easily identified. It is when someone physically hurts another person by punching, pushing, slapping, kicking, physically trapping, or hitting with objects. **Emotional and mental abuse** is harder to identify and address. This type of abuse occurs when someone gets what they want by manipulating how their partner feels. Emotional and mental abuse leave the victim feeling insecure and horrible about themselves, as if they deserve no better, which makes it hard for them to end the situation. **Verbal abuse** is when a person constantly attacks a person with words—using put downs, name-calling, and screaming. **Sexual abuse** happens if a person forces another to engage in a sexual act without that person's consent. If you or any of your friends are experiencing anything like this, it is important to talk to a teacher or counselor about it. Check out the back of this book for more suggestions on places where you can find help.

LET'S GET IT ON
Sex

CHAPTER 3

Sex, Sex, and
More Sex—Please

Here we are at the SEX chapter. Finally.

So why is it that most of us guys are more comfortable watching porn together in a group than having honest, functional conversations about sex and sexuality? Sex is personal and that's what makes it so hard to talk about. We're all scared to admit what we don't know.

When it comes to sex, there is so much pressure to fit in and show that you're a MAN who has it all figured out. But not knowing everything, feeling nervous about sex, and caring about your partner are all normal feelings. It means you're human. Let's face it, though, some guys are haters who will tear you down for speaking honestly, especially emotionally, about sex. That's why you hear so many guys bragging, right? It's safer to act like you're a stud who knows it all. But here's a tip: even those guys are a lot more nervous about sex than they're willing to admit.

Talking honestly about sex is a GOOD thing. Knowing that other guys have the same doubts as you can make you less nervous. Knowing how other guys acted in certain situations can make you more confident when dealing with sex. And bro, feeling less nervous and more confident is going to help you make smarter decisions about sex.

There are a lot of things that influence us about sex. Even though a lot of us say that we have our own mind and opinions, the truth is that we all need to learn more about sex in the real world. If you only get your information from porn then, damn, we are all in trouble! So read on...

SEX
Turn the lights down low...

Give Yourself a Hand!

Masturbation

and U

Playing with yourself. Jerking off. Choking the chicken. Whacking off. Whatever you call it, masturbation is something that crosses all our minds once in a while... or once every five seconds! I mean, knowing that you can touch your penis until you have an orgasm is kind of tough to forget.

Here's the thing: most of us masturbate even if we deny it or crack jokes about doing it. But just because most guys jerk off, doesn't mean every guy has to. Some guys just aren't interested in a do-it-yourself approach. Other guys are taught by their parents or their religion that masturbation is wrong or a sin. If you're not into grabbing some skin, that's your choice, bro. Hands on or hands off, it is completely up to you.

Whether you consider the deed dirty or delightful, here are a few interesting things to think about:

- Masturbation is the SAFEST SEXUAL PRACTICE. Zero risk of unplanned pregnancy. Zero risk of catching any sexually transmitted infections.

- Masturbation is not harmful. Anyone who tells you that you'll go blind, grow hair on your palms, or run out of sperm is full of shit. In fact, some studies show that masturbation may help prevent the development of prostate cancer.
- Masturbation can make you better at sex. Think about it. What better way to get to know your own body and what turns you on? A guy who can talk to his partner about what feels good is a guy who's gonna have a good time.

Masturbation
Myths vs. Facts!

"Hairy palms"
Uh. No.

"If you whack too much, you run out of sperm."
Your body is busy making more cum than you'll ever need. Don't worry.

"Masturbation gives you zits. Masturbation makes you need glasses."
Most people start jerking when they hit puberty, which is also when
you get zits and sometimes realize you need glasses. It's a coincidence.
Get over it.

"Nobody masturbates."
Many guys jack off regularly.

"Masturbation can give you sexually transmitted infections."
You can't give yourself an STI. I mean, duh.

"Only guys do it."
A lot of girls buff the muffin. A lot don't. Nobody's business but their own.

"Masturbation is for single losers who can't get dates."
Most men who jerked off before they were in a relationship keep jerking
off after they get into a relationship.

LIP SERVICE

Kissing

Lucas Perez

Kissing is an intimate experience. Often it is the first intimate physical act of a relationship. Some people place a lot of importance on the first kiss, believing that you can tell a person's true feelings from a kiss. Whatever you believe, I'm sure you'll agree that kissing is FUN!

There are many different ways of kissing. If you and your partner are looking for variety of the kissing kind, here are a few ways to try.

P.S. Always make sure, your mouth is clean before going in for that kiss. No one likes kissing someone who has bad breath. Brush those pearly whites and carry gum so you'll always be fresh and minty clean.

French Kiss
The most famous. Open-mouth kiss, with tongue.

Spiderman Kiss
My personal favorite. Like in the movie, you kiss upside down, your lower lip on your partner's upper lip. If you don't have a web to hang from, try lying on the couch.

Flavor Kiss

Put a piece of gum in your mouth, just before you and your partner French kiss. While kissing, pass the gum back and forth, and see how long it takes for the flavor to run out.

Vacuum Kissing

While in an open-mouth kiss, suck in deeply so you're sucking the air from your partner.

Pop Kiss

Use Pop Rocks candy.
Explosive open-mouthed kiss.
Need I say more?

Tongue Tease

While you're French kissing, pull back slightly and flick your tongue up and down quickly while your partner is doing the same.

Baby Kisses

Short, soft, and sweet kisses that build up to full-blown locking of lips.

Taste Test

When in the midst of French kissing and the opportunity presents itself, take control of the situation in a sexy and tempting way by gently sucking on the tip of your partner's tongue.

To Be a Virgin or Not to Be a Virgin...

Lucas Perez

Some guys see their virginity as the only thing they'd like to lose. For other guys, keeping their virginity until they get married is important to them. Whatever a guy believes, it's interesting to know how he defines "virgin." We asked around and got a list of activities that guys meant when they said they'd first had sex:

- first sexual intercourse
- first orgasm during intercourse—"Look Ma, no hands!"
- first sexual touching
- first orgasm from another person
- first oral sex experience
- first anal sex experience
- first enjoyable sexual experience

We also found out that there are a lot of other "firsts" that are important to people:

- first crush
- first relationship
- first kiss
- first time in love
- first fight
- first breakup
- first pregnancy scare

Whatever "first" defines your virginity, remember that it is YOURS, to give away or to keep!

SEX *Do Ya Really Need It?*

Andrew Coimbra

Okay, so throughout this book, you'll learn about how to protect yourself from big bad wolves known as STIs and how to *not* get a girl pregnant by accident. Important stuff, but one of the most important things anyone could ever tell you when considering sex is this: You don't have to have sex!

Just because you've got the urge, doesn't mean you have to do the deed. And just because your best friend Jimmy has sex, like, every other day (and talks about it constantly), doesn't mean you have to! I mean really, if Jimmy jumped off a bridge, would you?! I would HOPE not. Jeesh. 'Cause having sex is kinda like jumping off a bridge. Sure it's a thrill, but you can never be sure what's at the bottom.

Abstinence, or not having sex, could be one of the better things you could do to protect yourself.

Check it out:
If you are not sexually active…

- you are at zero risk of getting HIV/AIDS from sexual contact.
- you don't need to worry about them other pesky STIs.
- you don't need to lie when your mom asks, "Have you done the 'Dirty Deed,' dear?" (Ew. Embarrassing).
- you don't need to keep dirty secrets from your friends, thus ruining amazing friendships.
- you can feel better that you're not giving into peer pressure, media pressure, or hormonal pressure—you, my friend, are an individual!

The First Move

Ah, the challenges of making the first move...

Making the first move on a girl can be very stressful and hard to deal with. You gotta feel within yourself that the time is right, but you gotta be down with whether or not your G is ready too. You may think that it's time, but if your G decides that she's not ready, you better relate, not hate. If you ask me, girls can be very sometimes-ish: Sometimes a girl can make you feel like she wants you to make a move, and at other times that same girl can make you feel like shit. Nobody wants rejection, yo, but if you do get a "no," deal with it—don't be a dick about it. But if you get a "yes"... oh, man! Sweet success.

No matter what happens, you're gonna feel mad nervous around a G, and you won't know how to make that first move. You don't have to tell me that it feels mad crazy, yo, but it's just the way it is. It's a part of life and we all got to live with it. Bottom line: guys, make sure before you make the first move that you and your G are truly ready.

Not Sure...

Kyle Brandos

When I got my first serious girlfriend, I felt amazed that sex was suddenly an option for me, but I was also worried about it. We would make out and fool around but always stop before it went further than kissing and touching. When my girlfriend talked about sex, I told tell her that we should wait 'cause I wanted her to be sure. I tried to make it about *her* not being ready, 'cause I felt that, as a guy, *I* should always be ready. But, really, I wasn't ready. I didn't know if she was "the one." I wanted the first person I had sex with to be someone I was going to be with for a long time. I also didn't want to sleep with her and later, if we didn't stay together, have her feel like I was some asshole just using her for sex. I just didn't want to be responsible for that.

First Time

Conrad Begari

I remember the first time I had sex like it was yesterday. I really wanted to have sex because I really liked my girlfriend. We had a tough time deciding if we were even going to do it since we were both virgins—the anticipation of us both losing it was scary.

After a while of thinking it over, we decided having sex would bring us a lot closer to each other, and we quickly started acting. On the day that we did it for the first time, I was concerned about her mom catching us in the act so my heart was beating very fast.

We were finished minutes later. Yup, minutes. First time, what do you expect? Even though it didn't last long, it met my expectations 'cause it felt so good for me. But not for her. She said it was painful and she didn't like it so much. She even started bleeding a little. At the time, I didn't understand why. It turns out it happens to a lot of girls when they lose their virginity. It comes from some tissue called a hymen that covers their vaginas and get broken during sex. I was glad to know the bleeding was nothing to worry about.

After that first time, whenever we had sex, it was a lot more enjoyable for both of us, instead of just me.

First-Time Fears

Lil Dirrty, 15

The first time I had sex, I had all these expectations about what I was gonna do, what she was gonna do, and how long I was gonna last. There is a lot of pressure going into sex to be good at it right away. But you know what? You just can't plan these things.

What you can plan is how to protect yourself. My biggest fear about having sex for the first time was getting an STI or getting the girl pregnant. I made sure we used a condom. When you are getting ready to have your first time, or any time for that matter, be sure to wrap it up with a condom!! You don't need any nasty infections or little mini-you's running around.

Before We Had Sex

Anonymous, 17

It was a simpler time, before I first had sex. There was just so much less to worry about. All I was concerned about was that I had feelings for a friend, and that she was beautiful. We could talk for hours, about anything...the weather, songs, our families. It didn't matter. My friends told me "You're soft, man...why haven't you hooked up with her yet?" I tried not to care about what they had to say, even though I thought they did have a point.

But soon she and I began to grow closer and so did our bodies. We started to touch. First, we just held hands, and then our lips met. This continued for a while and then we got more serious. My hands would explore her body and hers mine. I'd touch her face, her breasts, and her booty. Eventually, my hands would go down below. She'd squirm with anticipation when I touched her.

For a while it was great. That's all we needed. We were comfortable with each other. I didn't need sex; however, one day, the sex conversation came up. She wanted to—you could even say she was eager. I, on the other hand, well, honestly I was afraid. I had so many questions. What if the condom breaks? What would happen if we became pregnant? I was worried, so I talked to a few people about it. Some said I should wait. Some said to do it. Everyone said, if I did it, to use a condom.

I chose to go for it. We decided to do it when her parents went away for the weekend. I'd bring the condoms. That night, we were in her parents' bed and then I was inside her and...wow. I don't know how to explain it, just wow.

The next few weeks were chilling. We had sex several more times. But, eventually we started arguing about little things. Then our fights increased in number and in size until one day neither of us could stand it. We had once made each other extremely happy, but now we made each other extremely sad. We decided to have a break from each other. I don't really believe in breaks because they always eventually lead to breakups, and this situation was no exception.

I'll always have a place for her in my heart, but one can't live with the past forever. In the end, it worked out for the best. We still talk and I still have no regrets. I'm glad we had sex and that there was never a problem with the condom. 'Cause even though we never had a pregnancy scare, we still broke up— how would we ever have handled getting pregnant?

First

Anonymous, 16

We started as friends and then it became
Stronger
We spent a lot of time together and then our
time got longer
I noticed things were different between us
because we started to touch,
I know the feelings got stronger without your
touch I missed so much
When we were alone the things that went
through my mind, Your soft lips against mine,
For sure, I knew you were mine,
we kissed and caressed,
you rub up on my chest and then I knew for
sure.
You stopped and locked the door...and then it
began,
you unbuttoned and then you unzipped until I
was fully bare. You on top of me, the pressure I
felt and that's when I became scared
the things you whispered in my ear had me
weak as day. You inside of me

body to body and then we began to play.
Tears drizzled down my face and you wiped it clean,
Shivers through my spine I felt as I moaned and screamed, the gentle touch of your hands made me feel secure.
A feeling words can't describe it was impossible to ignore. The night lasted until day, I need say no more

An

Unsettled
Mind

Anonymous, 18

I am gay. As much as I would like to fully express myself to society, it is often very hard for me because of the experiences I had growing up in the Caribbean. I always knew that I wanted to be with men, but where I grew up, it was (and still is) said to be wrong. I was always taught that it's sick, perverted, sinful, and abnormal to feel an intense love for someone of my own sex. But even in my youngest days, I always played with the boys and never had an interest in girls. As I got older, the one friend who I would always talk to was a guy. He eventually became my partner.

We were together for four years while I attended high-school. Our relationship was a secret because the finger-pointing and threats were too much for me to handle. But our secret must have been discovered, because he was gruesomely murdered for being gay. I had to flee my country, fearing for my own life.

Even in countries where being gay is more accepted, it is not easy to discover that you are gay. There are always people, even your friends, who make it very clear what they think of being gay by telling terrible jokes, promoting hurtful stereotypes, and spreading hateful misinformation. It's no wonder that you might choose to hide your same-sex feelings from others. You might even try to hide them from yourself.

The big question is "Am I normal?" Well guess what, yes, you are normal. There have always been people who are attracted to members of their own sex, regardless of whether or not this was accepted by their society. But it's not right that anyone should have to suppress their real feelings because of this prejudice. It's normal and healthy to be yourself, whether you're lesbian, gay, bisexual, or heterosexual. I don't believe people decide who they fall in love with. I didn't choose to be gay; it's simply who I am. **I just wish I could always be myself without ever being AFRAID.**

Experimentation

Myke Anderson

I think that anytime we masturbate, we're experimenting. We're finding out what things turn us on. Even if you think you know what gets you off already, there is probably still more you could learn, right? Variety is the spice of life and all the nerves in your body can make for some pretty spicy sensations.

Think about your chest. Guys have nipples too, right? Just like with girls, the nerves in your nipples are very sensitive. Try playing with them and you may be surprised how good it feels. Or maybe you hate it. Either way, once you figure it out for yourself, you'll be able to tell your partner exactly what you do and don't like.

What about your butt? A lot of guys are totally afraid of their own ass. Sure, it's your body's waste dump, but so's your penis and

that hasn't stopped you from touching it. Your anus is another place where the nerves are ultra-sensitive. You might try rubbing it to see how it feels. Just wash up before you eat anything!

If you just want to stick with your dick, you can still go for variety. Try different kinds of lube while masturbating—like hand cream, baby oil, or even your own spit (these work as lubrication when you're solo, but are damaging to a condom when you're with a partner. Pages 105–106 have more info about lube). Try different materials: some guys like wearing a glove, other guys use pillows, and still other guys prefer using a plastic bag full of lube. It's your choice. You can also try different positions: standing up, lying down, sitting in a chair, crouching, whatever. Try different locations: in the shower, in the bathtub (underwater!), or even outside (in private, duh).

Most people never get all the pleasure they can get out of sex because they never experiment. You don't need to get totally freaky, but try out some new tricks. If you don't like it, go back to what you like doing. And remember: if you can tell your partner your likes and dislikes, you'll make the most out those times when you're not flying solo.

GOING DOWN?
All About Oral Sex

Blow job. Eating out. Giving head. Whatever you call it, oral sex is any sexual activity involving the mouth and the genitals. If you want to get all technical, *cunnilingus* is oral sex performed on a lady, and *fellatio* is oral sex performed on a dude.

Now, a lot of folks, both guys and girls, think that oral sex is a safe way to have sex and avoid pregnancy and sexually transmitted infections. Well, I got news for y'all: oral sex is a sexual activity with risks!!! Okay, yeah, you *can't* get pregnant from giving or receiving oral sex, BUT there *are* many STIs that can be passed on through oral sex. Did you get that?

YOU CAN GET AN STI FROM ORAL SEX!

Now that we're clear, I'm gonna tell you that there are ways to protect yourself from STIs if you are having oral sex. Gentlemen, prepare to get your latex on.

Blow Job Security

Okay, if you are going to be giving or receiving a blow job, always use a condom. It's like this: STIs that can grow on your penis can also grow in your mouth and throat. Nasty. What that means is you are just as at risk of catching an STI receiving a blow job as giving one! So use a condom.

Yeah, I know—many people don't like the taste of latex. Well check this out: you can get flavored condoms. No joke. Condoms come in a crazy variety of flavors like strawberry, grape, lemon, and chocolate. Who doesn't like chocolate?

Okay, okay, I can hear some of y'all saying, "I don't like using a condom 'cause it dulls the feeling in my dick." There are thinner condoms available, but do your homework to find out whether or not it's a decent brand and whether it's right for you. Thinner condoms may be more likely to wear or break. Otherwise, consider this: some guys actually don't mind if they feel a little bit less 'cause it makes 'em last a whole lot longer.

Important safety tip: never use a condom with nonoxynol-9. (The name will be on the package.) That stuff is a spermicide that can cause numbing, burning, and irritation of the mouth. Not fun. Oh, and if you or your bj buddy are allergic to latex, buy yourselves some condoms made from polyurethane. Check your local drugstore.

Eating Out in Safety

Now, if you are going to be going down on a girl, you should always use a barrier between your mouth and her vagina. I'm not talking

about no Great Wall of China or anything, but you need something to block that two-way street of sexually transmitted infection. Yup, STIs can be passed between the vagina and the mouth just like they can between a dick and mouth. So what do you use?

Your best bet is something called a dental dam. I hear ya saying, "Damn! What the hell is that?" A dental dam is a thin sheet of latex that you hold against your lady's vaginal area while you do your licking. They're called *dental dams* 'cause dentists use them when working in people's mouths. So you know they're safe—but trust me, they feel a lot better for sex than during a visit to Dr. Drill.

Problem is, dental dams can be difficult to find. But guess what? You can make your own. Arts and crafts time! Take a new non-lubricated condom, cut off the bottom and the tip, slice it open, and then spread it out so you've got a rectangle of latex. Boom! Instant dental dam. You can also cut up a clean latex glove—just be sure you have a piece big enough.

Again, if you don't like the taste of latex, you can get flavored dental dams or you can make one out of a flavored condom. Again, never go licking any product that contains nonoxynol-9 (check that package, man!). And, again, if you or your partner is allergic to latex, use polyurethane.

So what have we learned? Dude, you gotta suit up before going down. Every time.

YouLube–
Top 10 Things to Know about Lubricants

Lube is short for lubricant and can make sex more pleasurable. Because sex can involve lots of body parts rubbing together, lube is a safe way to reduce friction that can cause irritation and pain. There are, like, a hundred different kinds of lube out there, or your local drugstore may only have a few. Either way, it is important to know some things about the stuff so you choose one that is right for you and your partner. Here, then, are the top 10 important things to know about lube:

1. **Natural Lube:** A woman's vagina produces its own natural lubricant when a woman is turned on. The amount of lubrication is different from woman to woman. Using additional lube that you buy in a store is okay and may be necessary.

2. **No Natural Lube**: Unlike the vagina, the anus (of both men and women) does not produce any natural lube. No lube means lots of friction, which means high risk of torn condoms, scraped skin, and sexually transmitted infections. So always use lube if having anal sex.

3. **Lube on Lube**: Lubricated condoms come with lube already on them. It's okay to use additional lube if you want, and it's especially a good idea for anal sex. It is always good to have extra lube standing by just in case!

4. **Designed for Sex**: Only use store-bought lubes that are supposed to be used for sexual activity. Never use home-made lubes or other products not intended for sex (like hand cream or baby oil—unless you're flying solo). Spit is not lube, despite what you may have seen in porn!

5. **Check the Ingredients List**: Know what you're getting into and what's getting into you. It's a good idea to compare lubes and choose one without any risky ingredients. So...

6. **Allergy Alert**: Look for any ingredients that you may be allergic to. If you find one, don't use that lube.

7. **Sugar-Free**: Stay away from lubes that contain any type of "sugar" or "glycerin" (flavored lubes especially have these). Sugars can increase the risk of some infections, such as yeast infections in women.

8. **No Oil**: Never use a lubricant that is oil-based (such as petroleum jelly). Oils break down latex and will eat through condoms. Condoms with holes don't work so great! Always look for water-based lubricants.

9. **Avoid Spermicidal Lubricants**: These contain harmful chemicals that can irritate the mouth, penis, vagina, and anus—so placing you more at risk for STIs.

10. **No Numbing**: Many lubricants are advertised as helping to "prolong pleasure." Be cautious of these products. Often these lubricants actually use numbing ingredients that make the mouth, penis, vagina, and anus less sensitive. But this will also numb any pain you may experience. Pain is our body's way of warning us that damage is being done, and that is something you definitely want to know!

WT(butt)F?

About (Anal) Sex

Myke Anderson

WARNING: Anal sex is against the law in Canada if you are under the age of 18. Federal courts have ruled that this law is unconstitutional, but the law hasn't changed yet. In the U.S., anal sex was illegal in some states until the Supreme Court overruled those laws in 2003.

Newsflash, guys: anal sex is not just something gay guys do; in fact not all gay guys do it; in fact, many straight guys *do* do it (so to speak). Why? Because for men, there are a ton of nerve endings in the anus and the prostate gland, which is located near the anus. All these nerves can provide pleasure to a guy when they are stimulated. Many men experiment with different kinds of anal sex to see if any feel good. Different strokes for different folks, as they say, so some people get the most pleasure out of having anal sex with a man, some people with a woman, and some guys all by themselves. Some guys dig the feel of a dick, others prefer fingers, and still other guys like to use sex toys. Maybe all of the above is what floats your boat. Whatever activity you might or might not be into, you gotta know that anal sex can be a high-risk activity so it is important to know all the facts.

Let's start with the anus (asshole, butthole—those are other words for it; I'm not calling you names). Unlike the vagina, the anus does not produce its own lubricant. This is not a place where you want dry friction, so plenty of store-bought lube should always be used. (Check out the piece on lube on pages 105–106.) The anus is surrounded by very strong muscles, called sphincters, that keep the anus closed. These muscles will automatically clench if anything is inserted into the anus. Trying to force anything in while the muscles are tight will literally be a pain in the ass. Going slowly and learning how to relax these muscles can reduce that pain. It may take some time before you are able to insert larger items, such as a penis, into the anus, so be patient—never force anything in there!

Compared to the vagina, which is quite elastic, the anus is a tight-ass. The walls of the rectum, the area just inside the anus, are fragile and can tear easily. That's what makes anal sex such a very high-risk activity for STIs. Any scrapes or tears can expose your body to STIs by allowing the infections to enter your bloodstream directly. This is one reason why lube is so important. Bottom line (so to speak): this is risky business, so it is crazy important that you know how the anus works before you even *think* of having anal sex of any kind.

If you *are* going to try anal sex, whether you are using your fingers, your penis, or a sex toy, always always always use a condom and lube. If you use a sex toy, put a condom on it, wash the toy between uses, and make sure you *only* use toys designed for the anus—these will have a broad base so that they can't get lost in your rectum. (Waiting in the ER with something stuck up your ass is a nasty way to spend a Saturday night.) And guys, if you are planning on giving anal sex to a girl, sperm may still enter the vagina, SO PREGNANCY IS POSSIBLE! Just another reason to always, always, always wear a condom during anal sex. Have I mentioned that you should always wear a condom during anal sex?

There are some other important safety tips to keep in mind when having anal sex:

- Always, always, always use a condom.
- Never use an oil-based lubricant, such as petroleum jelly. Oil breaks down the material in latex and will basically eat holes in your condom.
- Never use lube that contains nonoxynol-9, other spermicides, or any chemicals that numb. This stuff will irritate the anus and rectum and make it more difficult to tell if you are doing any damage.
- Avoid using lubes with sugar or glycerin 'cause they can make you more likely to get bacterial infections.
- When pulling anything out of the anus, make sure the condom is still on. The sphincter muscle will hold on tight and you don't want to lose a condom inside your rectum!
- Anal sex can be messy so be prepared. Lube and fecal matter (that's poo, dude!) can form an unpleasant liquid. Be sure to wash thoroughly after sex.

Follow these rules, and you'll have the safest possible experience with anal sex. No ifs, ands, or buts (so to speak) about it.

One-Minute Man
QUANTITY VS. QUALITY

Imogen Birchard

We thought that you guys would benefit hearing this from a woman's perspective, so here it is! You guys have heard it all before..."one-minute man," "premature ejaculator," trigger happy"...all those sort of things. Guys have it in their minds that if they cum fast, they're a bad lay. Well, ya know what? Some girls like long sex. Some girls don't.

The thing is, a girl needs to be turned on to enjoy sex, right? When we're turned on, we produce a natural lube in our vaginas, but that has to happen BEFORE intercourse, got it? It's called foreplay. So make sure you give a girl a lot of lovin' before sex: caress her, make out with her, eat her out, finger her—whatever she likes. I'd much rather have an hour of foreplay and only a few minutes of intercourse than the other way around. The thing is, if you give only five minutes of foreplay and an hour of sex, a lot of us girls will go dry, intercourse will become painful, and we will just want you to stop.

Now don't get me wrong here—we don't want it all over in two seconds or anything. But just don't think that longevity is what it's all about. Talk to your girl and figure out what's most pleasurable FOR YOU BOTH!

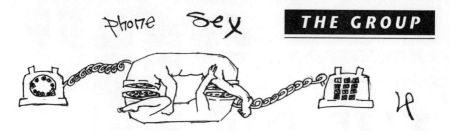

Phone Sex

You Don't Always Have to Hit a Home Run

Talking about sex doesn't always mean talking about inter-course. If you are looking to be intimate with your partner—but don't want to go all the way—get creative! Here are some other activities you might try.

1. **Flirt:** Use good old-fashioned conversation with something hot simmering beneath.
2. **Food:** Make your partner a fabulous dinner.
3. **Fashion:** Wear something sexy (or take off something sexy) for your partner.
4. **Fantasy:** Talk or type your hottest thoughts to each other over the phone or internet.
5. **Kissing:** Let your lips do the walking.
6. **Touching:** Let your fingers do the walking.
7. **Massage:** Slowly explore each other's bodies with just your hands.
8. **Shower:** Soap each other up and scrub each other down in the shower.
9. **Mutual Masturbation:** Lend your partner a hand while you get the same treatment.
10. **Oral Sex:** Not just for you! Don't expect to receive if you're not willing to give.

THE BIG "O"

Orgasm and the Ladies

Lucas Perez

How do you know if a girl had an orgasm? A lot of us guys want to know, right? Well I'm here to warn you: don't get too hung up on the question. For many people, the end result of sex is orgasm—you feel good and then you cum. For some people, sex is more about feeling good, and cumming may or may not be the end result. The thing is, if we spend too much time focusing on having an orgasm, we can miss the pleasure of getting there. So guys, the ride is just as good as the destination.

So you're gonna take the time to enjoy the ride, right? But I bet you still want to know: how can you tell if a girl has had an orgasm? Well, unfortunately, guys, we can't really but there are some signs. Obviously, when a guy orgasms, you get one big freakin' sign: he ejaculates. When a woman orgasms, the signs are more subtle 'cause her body can react in a number of ways. She may become flushed and her hips may contract or convulse. Her clitoris fills with blood and may become sensitive, but you won't be able to see that—only how she reacts if you're touching it. She may let you know verbally that she's cumming, by moaning or screaming. Or she might get real quiet. Each woman will have a different reaction when having an orgasm. Just as guys have different reactions besides ejaculating. Guys can moan, scream, and get flushed as well. Learning about your partner and communicating with your girl will help each of you know how to tell.

Now you're probably thinking, "Okay, I'll enjoy the ride and I'll watch for the destination, but how do I get her there?" Or you're just thinking, "How do I make girls cum?" Well, there isn't just one way to bring someone to orgasm. It may take different methods. For a lot of women, vaginal sex does not lead to orgasm 'cause they need more attention paid to the clitoris, which tends to get ignored during vaginal sex. The best thing to do is try to be aware of what turns your partner on. Try different things and see how she reacts. Listen to her and ask her what she wants.

Often guys think they have mad sex skills only if they can make their partners orgasm, and if they can't, they think they are bad at sex. But that's the kind of shit that leads some women to pretend to have an orgasm so they won't hurt a guy's feelings. If you are aware that your partner can still enjoy sex even without an orgasm and you are cool about it, she may be less likely to pretend.

Also keep in mind that some women have trouble reaching an orgasm. There are a lot of reasons for this. Sometimes it can be a physical thing, and sometimes it can be emotional. Physical reasons can be stuff like nerve damage, side effects of medications, and some medical conditions. Changes in hormone levels can also have an effect. Emotionally, it could be related to depression, stress, or negative past experiences with sex. Sometimes it can be because of how she feels about her body, or how she feels about the person she is with. Being nervous can also affect a person's ability to be aroused. You won't know about your partner unless you talk to her about it. Better to have it out in the open rather than go crazy thinking up reasons why she's not into you.

Where Is the G-spot?

First up, *what* is the G-spot? It's a spongy tissue inside the vagina that, if you stimulate it right, can drive your lady crazy with pleasure… Or maybe not—'cause not all women react the same way. Also, the G-spot can be difficult to find. MapQuest ain't gonna help you here, sucka! So here are some basic directions.

The G-spot is located a couple of inches inside the vagina, towards the front. If you insert your fingers and make a "come here" motion, you should be right around the G-spot. Generally, the best time is when she is really, really aroused and then you apply direct and consistent pressure to the G-spot. A G-spot orgasm can even cause some women to ejaculate a watery liquid. Don't freak if it happens—it's not piss.

Talk to your lady and explore together—she'll let you know what feels good.

Caught *in the Act*

Anonymous, 17

I was chilling with my girl in a park and we started fooling around. Things were heating up so I said, "You wanna hit my house and watch a movie." She happily agreed. I knew no one was going to be home at my place.

So, we're at my house all alone, watching a movie on my sofa. We started making out again and again shit started to get intense. My patio doors are glass so we decided to head up to my room. We walk in and I turn on the radio. She's already started to make herself comfortable on my bed. I looked at her, and she looked at me, and I thought why am I just standing here? So I got closer to her and we continued to do what we'd been doing downstairs.

Over the noise of what was now taking place in my bedroom, I thought I heard the door shut on the main floor. "Hold up for a second," I said. I listened for a minute, but I didn't hear anything so I just continued doing my thing. Little did I know, someone was climbing the stairs.

Then I heard my little nephew's voice call out from the staircase. "Uncle? What are you doing?" AWWW SHIT! was the first thing I thought. "GO AWAY!" I called back. I heard him step closer. The doorknob started to turn. I sprang into action! I jumped across the room, and with one thrust of my arms, I shut the door just as he was opening it. SMACK! The doorknob hit him in the nose. I heard my nephew cry and run down the stairs. I had to zip up and run downstairs to make sure he was okay. Man, my brother was pissed.

Getting caught having sex is more embarrassing than anything else, but it doubly sucks if a kid gets hurt because of it. Moral of the story: always lock the door when you're doing the dirty or find a place where you know you won't be disturbed.

The Young Tings

A Cautionary Tale

Anonymous, 17

It was a hot and steamy summer day. I was riding around on a bike when I noticed this young hottie walking down the street. So, I decided to try my luck. I caught her attention and she smiled at me. We started a conversation. She told me that she was on her way home and that she had just turned 16. I decided to try and get her digits so I wheeled along with her to the subway. We talked and laughed like two old friends.

When we reached the subway station, I got off my bike and asked for a hug. She took me in her arms and gave me a passionate kiss. She was about to leave when instead she said, "Let's go somewhere." I accepted her invitation.

I knew a perfect spot nearby where we could make out. There was a staircase under this dollar store in Chinatown that was hidden from prying eyes, but still well lit. It was a cool spot on a very hot day with a very hot girl. We started to kiss and hold each other passionately—and we ended up having sex.

After that, we spent the whole afternoon walking around hand-in-hand. It was great!

Over the next while, we made more arrangements to meet at various places around the city and usually ended up making out. Weeks started to pass when I began to realize that she often had trouble keeping dates, times, places. She wouldn't even bother to call or leave a message if she was late or unable to show up. I then realized that maybe this relationship was only sexual and wasn't going anywhere substantial.

Finally, after yet another time when she didn't show up, I saw a friend of hers on the street and asked her about my girlfriend's whereabouts. She replied, "Do you know she's only 13?" I couldn't believe it. I immediately knew I had to get out of that relationship.

The moral of the story: always, always make sure you know the real age of any girl you are with. Some girls look older than they really are and you don't want to mess around with someone who is too young. When it comes to meeting girls, there's enough to worry about without also facing problems with the law.

Age of Consent

In Canada, the law always views consent to sex from the perspective of the youngest person in the relationship. The following statements are in reference to the person who is the younger partner in a sexual relationship:

- A 14 or 15 year old can consent to sex with an older person up to **5 years older** (i.e., a 14 year old with someone up to 19 years old; a 15 year old with someone up to 20 years old) as long as the older person is not in a position of trust or authority (like a teacher or a coach).
- A 16 or 17 year old can consent to sex with an older person of **ANY age** as long as the older person is not in a position of trust or authority.
- It is illegal for anyone under the age of 18 to participate in anal intercourse, although some provincial courts have said this law is unconstitutional.
- An 18 year old is a legal adult and can consent to sex with an **older** person of **ANY age**.

In the United States, the age of consent differs from state to state, but nowhere is lower than age 16. Check out the Resources section for websites that can tell you about the laws in your state.

Be careful if any of this applies to your relationship; the law cares about age, NOT the way you feel about someone and NOT whether age matters to you and your partner. Even if you believe "age ain't nothing but a number," this doesn't mean the courts will agree.

Porn
*The **Good**, the Bad, and the Actuality*

Pornography. There's no shortage of the stuff out there. You got magazines, DVDs, video tapes, pay-per-view, and the good old internet. There's everything from simple, naked pics to the nastiest, dirtiest shit you never, ever wanted to imagine, let alone see. Some guys want nothing to do with any of it. Some guys want all of it. Most of us fall somewhere in between.

For those of us guys who like porn, we gotta realize that a lot of the stuff we learn about sex comes from what we see in porn. Yeah, we know it's "just a movie," but let's face it, we want to know what sex looks like and more importantly how to do it. Where else are we seeing people going at it? I don't want to totally knock porn 'cause I like the stuff, but it's worth taking a look at some of the good and some of the bad that porn might teach us.

The Good

Porn can show that girls can get off and that we can get them off.

- Porn can show that girls can like having sex and that sex isn't just about the guy getting off.
- Porn demonstrates that a guy can go down on a girl and they both can enjoy it.
- Porn shows that there are a lot of different positions that go far beyond missionary style. I'm not saying that you should do all of these, but there are some that you might want to try.
- Watching porn can also be a good way to release some tension after a long day, especially if you release some of that sexual tension by jerking off.

The Bad

- A lot of porn suggests that men need to dominate women and "show them who's boss." Being confident when having sex with a girl has nothing to do with pushing her down and slapping her ass. It's about respecting what gets her off as much as what does it for you.
- Porn often shows the guy coming on a girl's face to finish—a.k.a. a "money shot." That's fine if it's what you and your partner are into, but it's not how most sex ends in real life.

- Porn says that guys need to thrust as hard and as fast and as long as possible to give a girl an orgasm. In real life, that's not what most girls want. Ask your girl about what feels best for her during sex.
- Porn shows girls who cum over and over and over. In reality, it is not so easy for most girls to reach a single orgasm. It often takes foreplay and patience.
- Most porn doesn't show the use of condoms or anything else for safe sex. Unlike in the fantasy land of porn, you are at risk of STIs and pregnancy... especially If you have as much sex as they do in porn.
- Porn also shows us that sex lasts for a long time. Remember that porn uses all the tricks of the movies—acting, editing, even special effects—to create what it's showing. What you see is not just one long shot in real time.
- In porn, all the guys have huge penises and all the girls have large breasts, which suggests that you need to have a super-human body to be good at sex. Very few people look like porn stars and they still really enjoy sex.

THE ACTUALITY

Porn is porn; it's *not* real life. So watch it if you want, but don't follow it. There's so much more to actual sex, to how it really feels, to how to do it, and to what goes on inside your head than you'll ever see in porn. Check out the back of this book for websites that can tell you more about the real deal.

SEX *and* DRUGS
(Rock 'n' Roll Sold Separately)

Thinking of adding drugs or alcohol to your sex life to "spice it up"? Consider the facts before you do. Sure, drugs and alcohol can make you feel good and boost your confidence, but they can also make you stupid. Everybody's always telling us that sex is dangerous because of STIs, pregnancy, sexual assault, or even just losing your own damn self-respect. You don't want to prove them right (oh yeah, and maybe ruin your life) by making one bad call. So just keep in mind that being drunk and/or stoned makes you less able to make healthy decisions and more likely to use bad judgment. Not to mention that, if you use too much over time, you can cause long-term, even permanent, damage.

Long story short: if you use drugs or alcohol, make sure you protect yourself and know the facts:

ALCOHOL
Alcohol can make you horny (or even hornier than usual) and less nervous. Sounds great, right? But it also puts you at risk 'cause you might do things drunk that you wouldn't do if you were sober—stupid things like having sex without a condom

or even having sex you can't remember! Loosening up is cool unless you start making decisions you're gonna regret, like cheating on a partner or sleeping with your best friend's girl. And let's not forget that, even though booze may make you feel like a love-god, it is actually one of the leading causes of erectile dysfunction (your little buddy won't stay hard). Besides, you may feel sexy, but do you look it? A guy who takes his time, pleasures his partner, and doesn't drool all over the place is way sexier than you on your tenth beer.

DRUGS

Okay, so this isn't going to be a lecture on drugs—okay, well maybe a short one. We all know that drugs are bad for you and can even kill you. You've heard it all before. So, quickly, here are the facts on sex and drugs:

- Just like booze, drugs can make us feel horny, brave, and confident, but they can also screw with our judgment and encourage us to do things we'll regret.
- As with any drug, you may become addicted.
- Long-term drug use can mess with your health and your appearance. Nothing kills your sex life like looking nasty.

There is a crapload of different drugs out there, but here's a look at some of the more common ones.

Pot and Hash

Pot (marijuana) and hash (or hashish) have the same kinds of effects because they come from the same plant. Many of these effects are the same as the effects from alcohol. Taken in small doses, the stuff can make you feel sexier and may even increase how long you can go at it. But (and you knew there was gonna be a but), smoking up even more can quickly begin to change that. Too much pot or hash can make you depressed. You may not want to have sex at all or worse—even if you can get it up, you may not be able to feel anything during sex. And that's just short-term stuff. Long-term pot smoking can also make your body produce less testosterone. That means a lower sex drive, feeling depressed more often, and maybe even problems if you want to have kids one day.

Ecstasy

Ecstasy—or just "E"—can make you horny and feel like you have enough energy to have sex for days! Well, ecstasy is a stimulant, so yeah it increases your energy, but it also increases your heart rate and dehydrates you. That puts you in the danger zone for heart problems and overheating. Sex is already a workout for your body, so if you combine it with the effects of ecstasy, it's like red-lining the RPMs on a car. Don't get dead. If you're gonna use ecstasy, drink a lot of water and don't get too hot. Oh yeah, and this drug can also cause panic attacks and depression. And like all these drugs, overusing can stop you from getting hard. Ain't nothing ecstatic about feeling really horny but not being able to seal the deal!

Acid

Acid, or LSD, is a hallucinogen. Hall-o-what? It means that tripping on LSD makes you see and hear things that aren't really there. Sometimes these things make you happy, and sometimes these things scare the ever-loving-shit out of you. Trouble is you can't control which you're going to experience. The stuff you see may scare you so bad that you have a panic attack or lash out violently at yourself or someone else. This ain't so great for sex.

Crystal Meth

Crystal meth, also known as speed, is a methamphetamine. (If you can't even spell it, should you be using it? Just asking.) This stuff is a stimulant, like ecstasy, so it will also raise your energy, pump up your heart rate, and make you feel powerful. You might feel hornier, but there's the usual trade off—the effects of meth may make it difficult for you to cum. Sex can last a long time, but maybe not in a good way—we're talking possible chaffing of the penis here (ouch!). What's worse than a chaffed dick? How about a meth addiction? Methamphetamines are crazy addictive, which has a way of making your next fix more important to you than other things in your life, like sex, or, you know, eating food.

Cocaine

Coke is another stimulant. This stuff gives a shorter high so you may find yourself taking more and more to get the feeling you want. That's the road to overdosing. And—surprise, surprise—coke is another drug that can make it hard to get hard and even more difficult to cum.

Poppers

Poppers are all the rage among the club kids. Poppers provide a brief head rush and make you feel relaxed. Like booze, this may make you less nervous around the lads or ladies, but may also make you more likely to have sex you don't really want to have, not use a condom, or make some other mistake you'll kick yourself for later. Poppers also reduce your blood pressure, making you more likely to pass out, especially if you are any other medications or doing other drugs.

SUI

Sex While Under the Influence

Conrad Begari

When I first started wanting to get with girls, I had no idea how to go about it. I would talk to a girl at a party, feel good, and then get really nervous if it seemed to be going in my direction. I started smoking a joint and/or drinking beer to take off the edge and not be so nervous. It helped, so I started doing it more and more....

But one day in class, we talked about date rape. I heard about how some guys will be with a girl who wants to be there, but when she wants to stop, he forces her to have sex. I also heard about how guys under the influence of drugs or alcohol are more likely to make those kinds of stupid decisions. I thought about how I relied on being high or stoned to get with a girl, and I began to worry—what if, while under the influence, I couldn't tell if she was into sex or not? What if I was so out of it when I was with a girl that I couldn't remember what happened, and she started telling people something bad happened?

Maybe those worries were kind of extreme, but there was plenty of other stuff to worry about. In class, we also heard that when you're drunk, you might not have the judgment to use a condom. Or if you do, it could end up breaking and you might not notice. Even if none of that happens, if you are really drunk and you have sex, you may really regret who you had sex with. You might end up with someone you wouldn't even shake hands with normally.

Anyway, in the end I decided that I had to get used to getting up the nerve to be with a girl without drinking or smoking up so much.

Feeling
Consent

Antonio Giovanni Rumere and Lucas Perez

First of all, a lot of guys think that when their partner says "no," the partner is *actually* saying "yes." Well, guess what, you guys, you're wrong! "No" means no, and it will always mean no. It does not mean "maybe," "probably," or "later on." Continuing to have sex with someone who doesn't want to is not only humiliating and hurtful for your partner, it can also affect the rest of your life. Having sex with someone who says "no" is sexual assault. You could be looking at criminal charges, jail time, and a lifetime record as a sex offender, not to mention the guilt of living with what you did to the other person. So guys, make sure your partner wants to have sex and is capable of deciding that for himself/herself.

How do you know if you have consent?

We have one word for you...communication! **Talk** to your partner. Make sure your partner WANTS to have sex. Ask your partner and check in during sex to make sure your partner is *still* into it. As well as using talk, look for **non-verbal cues**. A partner who wants to have sex will be involved in it, kissing, talking, smiling, etc. A partner who doesn't want to be there will resist, not participate, or try to pull away. Sometimes people are afraid to say "no" because they don't want to hurt you or lose you. Make sure you don't give them the impression that, if they say no to sex with you, those things might happen. Otherwise, it's called **coercion**. Coercion means that you convince someone to have sex with you even though they don't want to because they are afraid of what might happen if they don't. Guys, you need to be careful because, if someone agrees to sex because they think they have to, then in the eyes of the law, you do *not* have consent. Also, someone needs to be aware of what they are doing in order to give consent. So if your partner is too drunk or high to know what is going on, your partner is unable to give consent. In this case, it is best to wait until your partner sobers up—you don't want to put yourself in a bad position...and we're not talking missionary.

What do you call having sex with someone without consent?

Having sex with someone without that person's consent is **sexual assault**. Sexual assault can haunt the victim for their rest of their life, causing anxiety and depression, and problems with their self-esteem. Being charged with sexual assault can affect the rest of your life. You could face a jail sentence and being permanently labeled as a sex offender—a record that follows you around until you die. No kidding. Sexual assault is an awful crime and a serious offense. Don't decide your partner's "No" is a "Yes." Don't ignore a "No" now even if your partner said "Yes" earlier. Don't put yourself in a situation that could be seen as sexual assault. Always make sure your partner wants to have sex. Always make sure your partner is not drunk, high, or passed out. Never make threats. If you have to convince someone to have sex with you, you are upsetting that person and putting yourself at risk. People should have sex with you because they are ready, they want to, and they are into it. Otherwise, back the hell off.

What should you do when your partner says NO?

That's an easy one...stop. Stop what you are doing immediately. Respect your partner. Don't try to convince your partner to keep going. Your partner may not be ready at this time. There is a myth that guys tend to think with their penis rather than thinking with their mind. When it comes to sex, you are in control of your body and you make your own choices. Don't think your behavior isn't your responsibility, 'cause it is!

What should you do if you are in that situation?

If you are the one who is told to stop, then stop. If you are the one who wants to stop, say "No." Make sure you are clear. Hold out your hands and say "No!" If the person ignores you, say it louder. Yell if you have to. If you need to use force, do so only to get away. Avoid putting yourself in situations where you may be in danger. Avoid getting so drunk or high that you may not be aware of what is happening or maybe not even remember. Guys can be sexual assaulted, too, so look out for yourself.

Check out the Resources at the back of this book for where to find more info.

Consent. Get it or get back. Got it?

Sex

Patrick Kabongo

Let's talk about sex, baby
If I don't get it, I'll go crazy
But while we in the position, hun
Since I'm naked, you might as well give me some
That's what's popping when we in the sheets,
    probably not love, but we as horny as can be
So when I sting like a bee
Let's hope the honey don't cum quickly
Oops, I forgot to put it on
I left it on my jeans right next to your thong
She said that ain't wrong
She said she wanted to feel me like emotions
So I put in the potion while we stroking
Her letting me do this to her made me very
Pleased in desire but Mary
Was too good at it to be a Virgin Mary
The way you freaking me well you making this virgin scary
But let's cut the bush down there, you hairy
After the sexing' I would like to marry you, but you don't
    feel the same, you just want to fuck and want me to
    forget your name
It's not insane
It's just not the same.

Me virgin you not, holl up, miss thang
I stroke a few times just to let go of my juices
No fruit punch, no the container is useless
So you tell me you loved it and you gotta
I respect you after the sex and didn't call you a ho
So you're gone and now we can go
Now flowing through the air like burning Hades
Some burning me, but no AIDS
Couldn't see it, hadn't seen her for ages
My finger on the Yellow Pages
Gave her calls like a referee, but she didn't answer
She gone like a dancer
Maybe this sex was a joke and my D.C. was the pranksta
Ring ring, someone belling up my phone
How did she get my cellie? She must have called my home
Saying how she wanna gimme head without the phones
And I said, "You can get this dog, hope you like the bone."
She said "Oh, so you remember me?"
Hell ya, girl, you that sexy g Mary
The girl that I gave it sexually
You were on top like stars on Christmas trees
And you were at the bottom like Jesus enemy
So she told me I want you to meet my friend and me
That's all good where do you want us to meet?
69-sheezer street
Got there, but what was I seeing?
a baby in her hands with its eyes gleaming.

What's the meaning
for all of this?
Come, gimme a kiss
and your baby
Huh? I know that's not my baby boo
we had sex once so the baby's whose?
What's the baby news?
If you don't take responsibility, my big daddy's scarred
And with his fist'll make me die hard
No, just come and settle this
Fists to fists, baby, I'll get the ring and we'll settle this
As it is when shit gets heated
I was Dallas and I was defeated so with baby I was greeted
This could be an impossible mission
This ain't no game, I took this position
So now I am in competition with myself and for sure
    I'm winning
My life long I could end it now even though the distance
Red pill, blue pill, I'll make my decision.

THE THIN RED LINE HIV/AIDS and Other Sexually Transmitted Infections

CHAPTER 4

No Lies, No Fear, Just Facts

First off, when we talk about HIV/AIDS and other STIs, we're not trying to scare the hell out of you. We're not here to tell you not to have sex or to make you think of sex as a terrible thing. But we are here to help you protect yourself. You gotta know that there are risks with all kinds of sexual activity. Like, did you know that you can catch an STI from oral sex? Or that you don't have to be a player to catch an STI? You can get one the *very first time* you share a sexual act with another person. So read on and learn how to protect yourself and reduce the risks. Understanding the basic facts about STIs is the first step in getting protected.

There are many STIs to watch out for, and this chapter will look at a bunch of them, but the one you've probably heard the most about is HIV/AIDS. AIDS is a huge issue around the world 'cause it spreads so easily if people don't use protection, 'cause it kills millions of people every year, and 'cause there is no cure, yo. And no matter what you might have heard, you need to protect yourself from it whether you are straight, gay, bi, or anything else. If you're human and you're sharing sex acts with another human, you're at risk of catching HIV and that leads to AIDS.

Yeah, STIs are some scary shit, but in this chapter we're gonna try to cut through the fears and the lies to give you the facts you need to protect yourself and your partner. And we're gonna look at the realities you might face when engaging with your partner. So many guys think that going "bare back" makes it feel better or shows that you trust and love the person. You can still love and trust someone but protect yourself, because no one is invincible. Even Superman had a weakness!

So have fun, be safe, and yes guys, here's that word again, communicate!

CONDOMS
at the Minimum

Myke Anderson

Right away we want to talk about condoms. Condoms are one of our main tools to protect us against HIV/AIDS and other STIs. If you are sexually active, always using a condom greatly reduces your risk of catching nasty infections and helps prevent pregnancy, too. But you gotta know how to use it. When you don't use a condom properly, it doesn't protect you properly, so knowing how it's done is as important as having condoms around.

Part of using condoms correctly is knowing what NOT to do:

- Do NOT store condoms in a place that gets really hot or cold. Too much exposure to heat can damage a condom, making it more likely to rip or even leaving holes in it. So don't keep a condom in your wallet; after a summer in your back pocket, that condom might as well have been kept in a sauna. And don't keep condoms in your car: it's an oven in the summer and a freezer in the winter.
- Do NOT use expired condoms. A condom has an expiry date, just like milk, written on its wrapper. Check that the date hasn't passed before you use the condom.

- Do NOT use a condom that is too tight. A condom should be snug, but not so tight that it might tear easily. Friction can cause a too-tight condom to break. There are condoms out there for every single dick size and shape. Find a brand and size that fits you well BEFORE you really, really need one.
- Do NOT use a condom that is too loose. Loose condoms slip off, duh. So don't buy the extra-large size just for your ego.
- Do NOT leave it behind. Soon after you cum, pull out but hold on to the base of the condom as you do. As your dick gets soft again, that condom is going to get looser.
- Do NOT use a condom without proper lubrication. Lubrication (or lube) is important to help to reduce friction. Most condoms are already lubricated, but you can also buy lube products separately. But never ever use oil-based lubes with a condom. Oil eats through latex. Condoms with holes in them don't work. (See "YouLube" in Chapter 3, pages 105–106, for more info.)
- Do NOT use condoms that contain spermicides (such as nonoxynol-9) because they can numb or irritate the mouth, vagina, or anus. Numbing or irritation can increase your chances of getting an STI. Again, see pages 105–106.
- Do NOT double up. Wearing two or more condoms on your penis at the same time does not give you more protection—IT GIVES YOU LESS PROTECTION! There is more friction between two condoms so they're more likely to break. It's the same deal if your partner is using a female condom: a condom on your penis as well will only cause more friction. One condom at a time, fellas.

- Do NOT double dip. Don't try to re-use a condom for a 2nd round—use a fresh one even if you didn't cum in round 1.
- Do NOT continue to use latex condoms if they irritate your skin or your partner's skin. Some people are allergic to latex. The good news is that you can find non-latex condoms in the stores. The bad news is that they have disadvantages over latex condoms. The most common non-latex condoms are made from polyurethane, but the stuff is more likely to break than latex. You can also buy condoms made from lamb skin, but they only protect you from pregnancy; they do not protect you from HIV/AIDS and other STIs.

So...

1. know what kind of condom to use
2. know how to use it
3. and use one EVERY TIME!

See "Wrapped Sausages" in Chapter 5, pages 206–208, for more info about how to put on a condom.

Making Condoms Your Friend

Myke Anderson

Using condoms doesn't need to be a hassle. In fact, they can become part of the pleasure. To get you and your partner started, here are some fun ways to use condoms that will keep things interesting:

PLAY A GAME:

Try these games and switch roles to make it even more fun.

Hide and Seek—Hide a condom somewhere in your room for your partner to find. Say "hot" or "cold" as your partner gets closer to the condom or farther away. For each "hot," you take off a piece of clothing. For each "cold," your partner has to take off a piece of clothing.

The Pat Down—Blindfold your partner and hide a condom somewhere in your clothing. Ask your partner to do a hands-only body search to find the condom.

Hands Free—See if your partner can put the condom on you without using hands. How? Feet maybe? Mouth?

Hands On—Ask your partner to put the condom on you using hands but blindfolded. Or maybe try being blindfolded yourself, with your partner putting the condom on you as sloooooowly as possible.

FOR ORAL SEX:

Try using flavored condoms—they can be a lot of fun. They come in flavors like peach, mango, chocolate, vanilla, berry, and many more. (Be aware that using flavored condoms for vaginal sex can cause irritation for some women.)

MEET LOCAL DISEASES
IN YOOR AREA!

The Gifts that Keep on Giving
Sexually Transmitted Infections

Sexually transmitted infections (STIs) are infections that you can get from having sex with someone who is infected. Well, duh. What not everybody knows, believe it or not, is that STIs can be passed through *any* sexual contact. So, if it involves any combo of penis, vagina, anus, mouth, fingers, or sex toy – and it ain't a solo performance – you'd better listen up. Remember, Romeo, anyone can pass an STI to anyone else so it doesn't matter if you are having sex with guys, girls, or both.

You usually can't know if someone has an STI just by looking at them, so you gotta use condoms and other forms of protection to help protect yourself. Knowing what STIs are out there can help you avoid them, detect them, and/or treat them. We know you've heard all this stuff before in health class, but here it is again in convenient book form 'cause who wants to put a hand up and ask the teacher, "What do you think these warts on my balls could be?"

So have a good look through this handy STI guide. At best, you can someday answer a Jeopardy! question. At worst, you'll recognize you have an STI but then you'll get it treated double-quick. If you do ever think you might have an STI, you should see a doctor right away. Letting an infection go untreated, can spell bad news for you health-wise.... not to mention anyone else you have sex with. Also keep in mind that, while some STIs can be treated and they go away, other STIs are with you for life, brother. They may not give you any serious problems, but you have to take care of them and you have to take extra precautions so that you don't infect other people.

If you do contract an STI, you gotta straight up tell your partner—and anyone else you have had sex with. They will need to get tested and treated. People show symptoms differently and sometimes women show symptoms that men don't or men show symptoms that women don't. Don't assume that your partner will know about having an STI. If you have an STI, suck up your embarrassment, be a man, and let your partner know. Wouldn't you want to know?

Bottom line: STIs aren't fun, so why even risk getting one in the first place? Always use a condom and any other form of protection you can. You don't want the hassle, reputation, or embarrassment of having an STI.

THE USUAL SUSPECTS

There are many different STIs out there that you need to know about and protect yourself from. Some are caused by bacteria, some by a virus, and some are parasites (yup, bugs). It's good to know what these STIs are because

a) Jeopardy! remember? and

b) not all infections are passed on the same way—so that means not all protection works for all STIs. That's right, my friend. Pubic lice will just scoff at your condom use.

Here is a rundown of the most common STIs seen in guys and girls.

CHLAMYDIA

Hey. Baby.

What is it?

Chlamydia is caused by bacteria. It can cause pelvic inflammatory disease in a woman, which can prevent her from having children in the future. Guys, this infection, if left untreated, can also prevent you from ever having kids. Chlamydia is the most common bacterial STI in the world! Don't be common.

How do you get it?

You can get chlamydia through any sexual contact, whether it's oral, vaginal, or anal sex. Chlamydia can appear in your penis, anus, or mouth. Having sex without a condom puts you at risk. Chlamydia can spread to different parts of your body. For example, if you touch your eye after touching an infected area, the infection can spread. Chlamydia in the eyes can cause very serious problems including blindness. And people used to say jerking off made you go blind...

How do you prevent it?

You need to be sure to use a condom every time you have sex. In order to protect your mouth, you need to use a condom or dental dam for oral sex. Remember, many people don't know they are infected, so don't take someone's word about being STI-free. Even if they do know, they might "forget" to mention it.

How do you know if you have it?

Only some people have symptoms of chlamydia so, if you have *ever* had unprotected sex, you may have it. You should get tested every six months, or every time you get a new partner. (Don't worry, it's pissing in a cup—no uncomfortable swabs required!) Symptoms are different for guys and girls.

- Guys, you may experience itching or burning in your penis. There may also be a discharge coming from the tip. (If you have to ask "What's *discharge*?" then you don't have discharge.) Some guys experience a swelling of their testicles (balls).
- Girls may experience swelling and pain around the vagina as well as a discharge. They may also get a fever and lower back pain.

If you get this infection through anal sex, you may notice a discharge from your butthole as well as swelling or itchiness.

How do you get rid of it?

Chlamydia can be treated with a prescription antibiotic. In most cases, a single dose will do, but be sure to take the advice of your doctor. Chlamydia can be cured but you can always get it again. A better idea is to never get it at all.

GONORRHEA

What is it?

Gonorrhea is a bacterial infection. If left untreated, gonorrhea can cause serious health problems: in both guys and girls, it can prevent you from having kids. It can also spread beyond the genitals and mouth and into the eyes, joints, skin, heart, and brain. Any zombie movie will tell you that bacteria in the brain only leads to trouble.

How do you get it?

Like chlamydia, gonorrhea is spread through sexual contact whether it's oral, anal, or vaginal. So if you are having sex with someone who is infected, you may become infected yourself. Gonorrhea can also be passed from a mother to her baby during birth. Babies with gonorrhea can go blind.

How do you prevent it?

Use a condom every time you have sex. Use a condom or a dental dam for oral sex. A person may have it and not even know.

How do you know if you have it?

Some people will have no symptoms and will not even know they have it. If you do have symptoms, you may notice a burning in your penis or it may be itchy. Your testicles may get swollen and sore. Your anus may itch or bleed. Let's hope that, if your ass is bleeding for any reason, you're already on your way to see a doctor.

How do you get rid of it?

If you think you have an infection or if you had sex with someone who did, you should see your doctor immediately. The doctor will run a test on your pee. Once gonorrhea is diagnosed, it can be treated with antibiotics. This will get rid of it, but you can always get it again *so be careful*. Gonorrhea has built up a bad-ass resistance to some antibiotics, so be sure to follow up with your doctor. Always follow the doctor's instructions. Doctors went to med school. You didn't.

SYPHILIS

What is it?

Syphilis is a bacterial infection that, if left untreated, can cause some very serious health problems. Syphilis can affect the eyes, liver, heart, and brain. In some cases, without any treatment, syphilis can cause death. Al Capone died of syphilis, but that doesn't make it gangsta.

How do you get it?

Like chlamydia and gonorrhea, syphilis is spread through sexual contact whether it's oral, anal, or vaginal. So if you are having sex with someone who is infected, you may become infected yourself. Syphilis can also be passed from a mother to her baby during birth. Happy birthday, kid.

How do you prevent it?
For vaginal and anal sex, always used a condom every time you have sex. Don't have oral sex unless you use a condom or dental dam. Can someone have syphilis and not know it? You betcha.

How do you know if you have it?
Syphilis goes through four stages as it develops in your body. The first two stages are when you are most likely to spread the infection to someone else. The last two stages are more likely to do permanent damage to your health. In the first stage, a sore may form on your penis, anus, or in your throat. Beware, 'cause this "sore" is painless and goes away on its own, so you might think "Hey, I don't need to see a doctor." Instead of getting better, though, you get the second stage. Stage two occurs about three months after you get the infection; you may experience flu-like symptoms, hair loss, muscle and joint pain, rashes, fever, and swollen glands. Again, these symptoms may go away on their own, but the syphilis is just taking another break. In the third stage, you may not see any symptoms at all, but the syphilis is still attacking your body. If you still stay away from the doc, you may enter the last stage. In the last stage of syphilis, you could experience mental health problems, blindness, deafness, and even death. These can limit your future dating possibilities.

How do you get rid of it?

The test for syphilis can be done through a swab of the infected area or through a blood test. Your doctor will then prescribe antibiotics. This should take care of it, but you can always catch it again.

GENITAL HERPES

What is it?

Herpes is a virus that is from the same family of viruses that cause cold sores in and around your mouth. This is *not* a family you want to know. People who have genital herpes have outbreaks of sores on their genitals. These sores are highly contagious. After a while, they go away and the virus takes a nap, but sooner or later, it becomes active again, causing another outbreak. The number of outbreaks will vary from person to person, but be warned: once a person contracts herpes, he or she will have it forever.

How do you get it?

Herpes is contracted through skin-to-skin contact. This means that, if your skin touches an infected area of skin, you can catch it. Because herpes is focused around the genitals and mouth, the skin around these areas is at the most risk. Although cold sores and genital herpes are not the same virus, they are from the same family of viruses and so can spread sores between the mouth and genitals. You cannot get herpes from toilet seats, pools, or bathtubs, so don't try telling your mom that's where you caught it.

How do you prevent it?

This one is tougher. Using a condom will help prevent herpes, but because it is spread through skin contact, a condom may not cover enough of an area. Avoid having sex if you are having an outbreak. Avoid having sex with someone who is having an outbreak—you'll be able to see the sores. BUT... remember there is still a chance that herpes can be spread even between outbreaks, when there are no sores to be seen. Using a dental dam and latex gloves will also help reduce skin-to-skin contact. And who knows? Maybe you'll actually dig all that extra latex.

How do you know if you have it?

You may develop small blisters around your penis, testicles, butt, and/or anus. And what could be better than itchy blisters on your privates? How about *bursting* itchy blisters? How about bursting itchy blisters that leave behind painful sores? With the first sign of herpes, some people get a fever or headaches. Sometimes a slight tingling or burning will let you know an outbreak is coming on.

How do you get rid of it?

You can't. If you get herpes, congratulations, you have it forever. There is no cure. There are medications you can take to try to make sure your outbreaks aren't too bad, but that is the best you can do. And once you get it, you will *always* have to be careful that you don't infect other people. You don't want to have sex with someone and then the only thing they remember is the nice blisters you gave them...forever! If you have herpes, ask a doctor or nurse what you can do to manage it better.

HEPATITIS B

What is it?
Hepatitis B is an infection of your liver that is caused by a virus. Hepatitis B can develop into long-term problems such as liver disease and liver failure. Because your liver helps remove poisons from your body, you kinda want it in good working condition. There are few symptoms for hepatitis B so many people don't realize that they have it.

How do you get it?
This infection is passed on through sexual contact and through the blood. Oral, vaginal, or anal sex can spread the hepatitis B virus. Using dirty needles for drugs, piercings, or tattoos can also put you at risk.

How do you prevent it?
I bet you can guess. If you said, "Use a condom every time you have sex and use a condom or dental dam for oral sex," you're right! Also watch out for any sores beyond the areas you've already protected with a condom or dental dam—sores can provide access to your bloodstream, so cover up with latex gloves if you see sores. Also don't share needles, which is just gross anyway. If you are getting a piercing or a tattoo, make sure whoever does it uses clean equipment and new needles from factory-sealed packages. Just blowing on a needle before sticking you ain't gonna do the job. Remember, many people

don't know they are infected so don't take someone's word about being STI-free. There is a vaccine that can help prevent you from getting hepatitis B, so ask your doctor about it. Some schools offer vaccination programs—check your records to see if you've been immunized.

How do you know if you have it?

There are two stages of hepatitis B. Some people will only go through the first stage. In the first stage, you may experience flu-like symptoms while your body tries to fight off the infection. There is a chance that your body will kick hepatitis B's ass; if so, you will experience no further problems and will no longer be spreading the virus to others. However, some people will not be able to fight off the virus and they will enter the second stage. This means they still have the virus and can still transmit it although they will have no symptoms. Over time however, hepatitis B will start to kick ass. In stage two, hepatitis B will damage your liver and make you ill. If you think there is a chance you could have come in contact with the hepatitis B virus, then call your doctor.

How do you get rid of it?

You can't. You can wait and see if your body fights it off but remember, while you are waiting, you are contagious! And if your body fails to fight it off, you have it for life. Talk to your doctor about how to take care of yourself to prolong the health of your liver. A doctor will use a simple blood test to look for hepatitis B.

HIV

What is it?
This here is the big one. HIV is the human immunodeficiency virus. Basically, this virus attacks your body's defense system, making it difficult for you to fight off infections. HIV can lead to AIDS, which is acquired immune deficiency syndrome. AIDS is a group of symptoms (that's what *syndrome* means) that attacks the body and will kill you.

How do you get it?
Like hepatitis B, HIV can be spread through sexual contact and through blood. Oral, vaginal, and anal sex all put you at risk for HIV infection. Using dirty needles for drugs, piercing, or tattoos will also put you at risk. There are a lot of myths out there about who can get HIV, but the solid truth is that *anyone* can get HIV. Whether you are gay or straight or bi, male or female, rich or poor, left-handed or right-handed, a fan of soft rock or a metal-head, etc., *you can get HIV.* Women can also pass HIV to their babies through breast milk.

How do you prevent it?
Condoms. Sex. Always. Condoms or dental dams for oral sex. Be aware of any sores you or someone else might have that could provide access to the bloodstream. Also don't share needles. If you are getting a piercing or a tattoo, make sure it's being done with clean equipment and new needles from factory-sealed packages. Remember, people don't always know they are infected, so just 'cause they say they're HIV-free, don't necessarily make it so.

RROOAARR!

AIDs
- Single & Looking.
- Tall & Muscular.
- Likes long walks on the beach.
- Dislikes H.A.A.R.T (an HIV Treatment).
- Future Ambitions: Taking over the world.
- Currently Destroying: Most of Africa.

AIDS IN ACTION!

How do you know if you have it?

It can take many years for people to develop any symptoms of an HIV infection. A person who is infected (HIV positive) can spread it even though he or she doesn't have any symptoms. Often people find out about being HIV-positive because some other infection won't clear up or they have a routine blood test. If you think you have been exposed to HIV, you should get tested immediately. If you are having sex, you should get tested regularly. There are often anonymous clinics around that do the tests. (Read up on testing on pages 180–183 and check out the Resources section at the back of this book for info on how to find clinics.) Be warned that it can take up to three months after you catch HIV before it shows up on a test.

How do you get rid of it?

You can't. There is no cure for HIV. Once someone gets HIV, doctors will prescribe medications that can help prolong life and delay HIV turning into AIDS.

See "Risky Business: AIDS" on pages 166–170 for more info about AIDS.

HPV

What is it?
HPV is the human papilloma virus. This virus is the most common STI in the world. (*Don't* collect them all! *Don't* trade them with your friends!) HPV can be present both inside and outside your body. Genital warts are one of the types of HPV infection. HPV can also cause some types of cancer.

How do you get it?
Like herpes, you can get HPV through skin-to-skin contact. Oral, vaginal, and anal sex are common ways to spread the virus, but *any* close contact can put you at risk. This STI didn't get to be #1 by being shy.

How do you prevent it?
Using a condom will help prevent HPV, but because it is spread through skin-to-skin contact, a condom may not cover enough of an area. Make sure you try to protect any areas where skin-to-skin contact may happen in and around the genitals, the butt, and the mouth. Using a dental dam and latex gloves will also help reduce skin-to-skin contact. Avoid coming in contact with genital warts (like you need to be told) because they are super-contagious. There is a vaccine for women between the ages of 9 and 29.

How do you know if you have it?
Because there are so many different types of HPV, it's not an easy sucker to detect. Some of the types, such as genital warts and the types that cause cancer, leave symptoms.

- Genital warts are small bumps that can appear around your penis, testicles, scrotum, anus, and thighs—basically all the areas your boxers cover. Women can have bumps around their vagina, anus, and thighs.
- HPV types that cause cancer can produce lesions (sores) that doctors can test for cancer.

Many people have HPV and don't know it. Did we mention it is the most commonly spread STI?

How do you get rid of it?
You can't. There is no cure for HPV. Symptoms can be treated, but the virus remains. Sometimes, the virus goes away on its own. Warts can be treated but they will come back. People who develop cancer can be treated for the cancer, but the HPV remains.

PARASITES

PUBIC LICE

What is it?
Pubic lice are also known as crabs, but this ain't no trip to Red Lobster. These little bastards are tiny crab-like insects that nest in pubic hair. They are not the same as head lice, although crabs can also be found in hair on the chest, armpits, and face, including eyebrows.

How do you get it?
You can get crabs through close contact with any place where these things are hanging out. They have no wings so they need

to crawl from living on one person to living on another. During that journey, they can live for up to two days in clothing, bedding, and towels. Because of the areas they nest, sexual contact is the most common way for crabs to spread, but it's not the only way. Anyone can get crabs, and it isn't linked to being unclean. So don't think that, because a person is scrubbed and smells good, they don't have hundreds of little roommates.

How do you prevent it?
The only way to ensure you don't get crabs is to avoid getting close to someone who does. Don't share clothing, bedding, and towels with someone who has crabs. If you have crabs, don't have sex with anyone until you get rid of them. Wash all clothing, bedding, and towels. Dude, do that anyway.

How do you know if you have it?
The little insects can be too small for you to see, but you might see their grayish eggs stuck to your hairs or bluish spots on your

skin where they have bitten you. (When crabs bite you, they leave marks that are very itchy.) You might also see some tiny black lice droppings (yup, bug poo) in your underwear. Ain't nobody should be crapping in your gotch, not even you!

How do you get rid of it?

A doctor or nurse will be able to identify the tiny insects. You will then have to use a special shampoo to wash with. You will also have to wash your clothes, bedding, and towels. You can use a fine-toothed comb to pull out the eggs attached to your hairs. Crabs won't go away on their own. They won't find someone better and move out! You need to get treated.

SCABIES

SCABIES

Heh.
Heh.
Heh....

- Single & Always Looking.
- Small and Compact.
- Prefers a mate with a Home.
- Dislikes Shampoo from Doctors.
- Has a Pubic Hair Fetish.
- Future Ambitions: Taking over your Eyebrows.

What is it?

Scabies are tiny parasitic mites that actually burrow into your skin and plant eggs (ever seen the movie *Alien*?). The eggs hatch and the larvae travel to other parts of your body. Mites like more than the just genital area—they like *any* warm place on the body, so any area where your skin folds is a common home for scabies.

How do you get it?

You can get scabies from any close contact with someone who has them. If they can crawl from person to person, they will. Because sexual activity provides the closest contact, it is a very common way for scabies to spread. You can also catch scabies from sharing clothing, bedding, and towels with an infected person.

How do you prevent it?

The same way you prevent crabs. Avoid contact with someone who has them. Don't share clothes, bedding, or towels. If you have scabies, do not have sex until they are completely gone.

How do you know if you have it?

About a month after infection, you can experience itchiness and redness. You may notice a rash in the areas where you are infected.

How do you get rid of it?

A doctor or nurse can identify these mighty mites. You'll have to treat infected areas with a special lotion. You will also have to wash your clothes, bedding, and towels. Be sure to follow the instructions of your doctor.

TRICHOMONIASIS

What is it?
Trichomoniasis or trich (pronounced "trick") is not a treat. It's a microscopic parasite that makes its home in the genital regions of both men and women. A nice place to visit, but these things want to live there.

How do you get it?
Trich is spread through genital-to-genital sex, most commonly from the penis to the vagina. It is more common for girls to get trich, but guys can get it too, and they can spread it to their female partners.

How do you prevent it?
Use a condom every time you have sex, which, by now, you're doing no matter what, right?

How do you know if you have it?
Guys don't usually have symptoms but you could experience redness and soreness at the tip of your penis. Girls can experience pain while peeing or during sex, a discharge from their vagina, and a bad odor from their vagina. (Well, what do you expect? These things are parasites!)

How do you get rid of it?
Trich can be detected through a lab test that looks for the parasite. Once discovered, it can be treated with antibiotics. Even though you get rid of it, you can still catch it again!

STI Freestyle

Patrick Kabongo

Some dudes move loose, they ain't rocking no shoes
If you go barefoot in these women, you making
   the wrong move
Gotta be cool and try not to rush nothing
Cause you can get burned if it's a one-way with no u-turns
You can catch STIs where your flesh don't burn
Better put a Jimmy hat on, why you guys don't learn
That some girls been packing them germs for sure?
Make the right move and you won't get put in an urn.

Aint too many that plan with it
Transmitted
Ain't just the gays
Trans with it
Condom first
Sex second
Or no chance
With it
'Cause viruses making huge splash like divers is

So listen and work with
What you got like MacGyver did
Or you will soon know
What dying is
Going in raw
Dangerous like skydiving is
No parachute
No going bare
You better have a pair of shoes
Or prepare to lose
Cause once you in and you exit
If the virus in
No exit
Jimmy hat or forget it.

Risky Business: **AIDS**

Gordon McLean

Do you know what AIDS is? Most people actually know very little about AIDS other than that it can kill you. There are a lot of myths about AIDS out there. But if you don't know the bullshit from the facts, you're putting yourself at a greater risk of contracting the virus that causes AIDS.

THE FACTS

So, here's the deal: HIV is not AIDS. HIV is the virus that causes AIDS. You get HIV, and HIV can lead to AIDS. Okay? Okay. HIV actually stands for human immunodeficiency virus. Once it gets in your body, it multiplies by messing with your body's cells. How does it get in your body? By swapping fluids (like blood, vaginal secretions, semen, and even breast milk) with an HIV-positive person. Unprotected sexual activity and sharing needles are two ways to do swap fluids. Once HIV enters your bloodstream, it begins to beat the shit out of your immune system. A weak immune system makes it really difficult for your body to fight off illness and infections. If your immune system gets beaten badly enough, HIV can cause AIDS.

So what's AIDS? AIDS stands for…

Acquired Immune Deficiency Syndrome

Key word: *syndrome*, which means it's a shitload of symptoms and diseases that gang up on you. AIDS is like the Alamo for your immune system—your immune system defends the body as long as it can, but eventually it gets so weak that it is unable to fight off disease. Many people with AIDS actually die of pneumonia or cancer.

THE BULLSHIT

Don't let anybody tell you that only gay men need to worry about HIV. The fact is, in the U.S. and Canada, the fastest growing group of people being infected with HIV is young women. The fact is that *everyone* is at risk of getting HIV. Gay men have been the scapegoat because HIV and AIDS were first discovered in North America when many gay men became infected. AIDS became a big topic, but doctors and scientists quickly discovered how HIV and AIDS spread and that it wasn't only gay men who were getting infected. But bullshit tends to stick, and some folks still think you can only get HIV if you're gay. Thing is, if you're straight and believe you are not at risk for HIV and AIDS, you're actually putting yourself in greater danger of getting it.

Whoever you are, you gotta know that there are many activities that put you at risk of getting infected. If you know what they are, you can better protect yourself. Read on, bro.

RISKY BUSINESS

On the next two pages are examples of activities that have higher, moderate, lower, or no risks of passing HIV. Remember that if something is listed as "low risk", it means there is still a risk. Don't take any chances. Protect yourself from *all* risky activities whether they are high risk, moderate risk, or low risk.

High Risk

- **Unprotected anal sex**—Sex without a condom allows fluid such as semen and blood to mix. Anal sex can often result in friction and tearing that opens up access to the bloodstream.
- **Unprotected vaginal sex**—Sex without a condom allows fluid such as semen, vaginal fluids, and blood to mix.
- **Sharing needles**—Sharing needles allows blood to be transferred from one person to another.
- **Unprotected vaginal or oral sex with a woman who is on her period**—HIV can be found in menstrual blood. This puts you and her at high risk.

Moderate Risk

- **Unprotected oral sex**—Oral sex is often seen as a low-risk activity but licking or sucking the penis, vagina, or anus *without protection* allows for fluids to mix. Any open sores in these areas or in the mouth will increase this risk. A recent trip to the dentist or even teeth brushing can make gums sensitive and sore.
- **Sharing sex toys**—Although sex toys don't have fluids of their own, if you use the same toy on someone else and then yourself, you are transferring fluids between you. Always wash sex toys between uses and use a new condom for each partner.

Low Risk

- **Kissing**—Kissing is a low-risk activity. HIV has not been significantly detected in saliva. However, any open sores, bleeding gums, or other access points to the bloodstream can put someone at risk.

- **Mutual masturbation**—Using your hands to masturbate each other or yourself is relatively low risk, but placing your hand on someone else and then yourself can pass infections. Any cuts on your hands or sores on your genitals increase risk.
- **Fingering**—Putting your fingers inside someone's vagina or anus is low to moderate risk. If you have any cuts or sores on your hands, your bloodstream is accessible. If you then put your finger in your mouth or in your own anus or genital area, you can pass infections. Use a condom or latex glove over your fingers for protection.

No Risk

- Stroking your partner's body in non-genital areas—such as the breasts, chest, head, legs, etc.—is safe as there are no bodily fluids involved.
- Massaging your partner in non-genital areas also has no bodily fluids involved.
- Touching or rubbing your partner through outer clothing avoids direct contact with bodily fluids. However, be careful of any fluids that may soak through clothing. Unless your underwear is made of latex, fluids and infections can seep through.
- Jerking off by yourself—hey, if you're touching yourself, you aren't sharing anything with anybody! Make sure your hands are clean.
- Phone sex. Get yourself and your partner off just by talking on the phone. Basically, it's jerking off to the sound of a sexy voice on the other end. No fluids exchanged. Finding a partner who likes phone sex is cheaper than those 1-900 numbers!!

Protecting yourself from HIV and other STIs is all part of taking care of yourself. Be sure to decrease the chances you will put yourself at risk. Here are some tips so you can be prepared:

- *Always* have condoms handy. If you find yourself in a situation with no condom, don't have sex. It may make for a crappy night but better than a trip to the doctor's office!
- Don't have sex if you are high, stoned, or drunk. People are less likely to protect themselves if they have been drinking and/or using drugs.
- If you are with someone who doesn't want to use a condom, let the girl or guy know why a condom should be used. Don't have sex with someone who doesn't want to use a condom or doesn't want you to use a condom.
- Anyone can have an STI. Just because someone is clean, says they don't have an STI, or has been with you for a while doesn't mean they aren't infected. Hygiene has little to do with STIs. Many people don't even realize they have an STI, so they think they don't have one. And people aren't always upfront about when they're having sex with other people. Protect yourself just in case.

Famous People with HIV/AIDS

Eazy-E
Original member of
NWA rap group

Anthony Perkins
Actor, *Psycho*

Freddie Mercury
Lead singer of
Queen

Makgatho Mandela
Son of Nelson Mandela

Sandra Bréa
Brazillian actress

Michel Foucault
French philosopher

My Uncle and My Hero in One

Anonymous, 23

When I was approached to help on the topic of HIV/AIDS, I felt very uneasy about it. To tell you the truth, I never wanted to write this story because of the pain it brings back to my heart. But I have found comfort in knowing that I'm not alone in experiencing the pain that AIDS causes in its victims and their families, so I hope my story might help someone else find comfort as well.

When I was growing up in the Caribbean, I looked up to my uncle. When I found out he was gay, I accepted him for who he was because he had always treated me better than my parents did. As a teenager, I was going through a difficult time, and later on I realized I had been trying to figure out whether I was gay or not. My uncle knew what was going on and helped me through it all. I could never thank him enough.

Much later, after I came to Canada, I learned that my uncle had contracted HIV. I didn't find out about it until it was almost too late. I went back to my country to visit him in the hospital. He was in good spirits and I thought he was going to be okay, but I guess I was wrong. The hospitals where I come from don't really have proper medicines for patients with HIV/AIDS. My uncle was discharged by the hospital with very little medicine to take—just a couple of puffers and some pills for anxiety. He didn't want my family to find out that he had AIDS, so he went to his home with no one to help him. He died a week later.

I was in total shock when I got a call from a family member and was told he had died. I am still very upset for what my uncle had to go through. He had to deal with his pain and suffering by himself because he didn't want anyone to know about it. He had no support from any of our other family members. I was, and still am, angry and hurt by this. It is a cruel world already, and no one needs to go through such a thing alone.

I will always admire my uncle for his strength and bravery. He was a good man and the best uncle I will ever have. He was very kind and gentle, and he always took care of others before worrying about himself. I miss him so much and I wish he were still here, but I do find comfort in the memories I have of him.

My **Bad** *Decision*

Anonymous, 18

I'd always thought that losing my virginity would be an amazing experience. Frankly, I thought it'd be like in the movies: boy meets girl…—or in my case, boy meets boy, boy falls in love, boy decides that other boy is worthy of being the first to enter him physically as well as emotionally (with protection, of course). I just thought it was natural that it would unfold that way. I'm not a stupid person. I make smart decisions in my life, but sex has a way of fogging your judgment for even the most important decisions.

You see, I was always the virgin. I was the one who nagged my non-virgin friends: "Don't go shagging yourself around town! AND if you do, always use a damn condom!" All my friends would put up with me because I was a sensible guy, and they knew that I wouldn't settle for some stupid one-time thing. I guess we were all wrong.

It all changed when one summer, for some strange reason, I suddenly started meeting all these guys who were interested in me. I mean, how do you go from nothing to, like, a whole bunch of guys talking to you? It's not like I was an ugly duckling!

Anyway, I suddenly found myself skanking-it-up, so to speak. I was meeting new guys and just fooling around a bit here and there—and I was totally happy with that, because I was finding myself and I was pleased with the results. And then I guess I started to get carried away; sex can be one dangerous tool, in more ways than one!

But I wasn't thinking about that when I met this one guy —over the internet, of all places. Now, I know all the stuff about being careful about who you meet online, but when you're a homo in your late teens, it's really not that easy to pick up other guys, trust me, so the internet comes in handy. Even so, when I met this guy, I made sure we chatted online and then over the phone for weeks and weeks until I felt comfortable with him. Of course, sex came up as a topic several times between us, but at first I only joked about it. Later, I told him that I was a virgin and that I had no intention of doing anything with him to change that.

Eventually, we arranged to meet. He had a car, so it was more convenient for him to pick me up. Well, one minute he was picking me up, and the next we were in a parking lot in the backseat of his car in our underwear. This was almost the worst part 'cause I don't even like stripping down to my undies for the doctor. How dare I do this—with someone I've only known in person for 15 minutes?!

Anyway, kissing, sucking, and touching went on for a bit, and then I found myself exposed to him and him to me. Next thing I knew, he was leaning over to the front to grab a tube of lube from the glove compartment. Even as he squeezed some lube into his hand, not once did I really think we were going to have sex. It's not that I didn't want to; I was so caught up in the moment—as people too often are in these situations—that I felt like I was up for anything.

Then he went in and my virginity was gone. It wasn't magical. There wasn't any pretty synthesized violin-type music playing. It was just the sound of our breath, the cars around us driving by, and the wind blowing. It sounds sexy and raw, but it was just *not* what I had dreamt of, and trust me, I'd dreamt of that moment in detail. You may also have noticed by now that I didn't mention anything about a condom. That's because he didn't use one—why? I don't know. I didn't even THINK about it at the time. If I didn't really think he'd stick his penis in me, then why would I think of needing a condom?

To put icing on this cake of love and joy, a week or so after we had sex (we had sex, he didn't make love to me), the bastard had the nerve to tell me that I'd lied to him about the fact that I was a virgin—OF WHICH was so true, I don't even know how to express to you how true it was. Anyway, I didn't see him again after that.

I'm not stupid and I don't usually make stupid decisions. Most of the time, I feel I'm a strong person, but I know now that I can have moments of weakness. Having unprotected sex with a near stranger was the most irresponsible thing I've ever done. Even though I'm very lucky to be clean and healthy, the whole experience is still something that I regret. I don't want to have to face living with that kind of bad decision ever again.

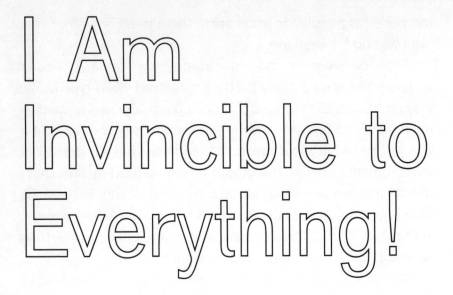

I Am Invincible to Everything!

Asha Blucher

There are always people out there who think that HIV/AIDS is not happening in their own community. This silence casts a shadow that can keep many at-risk people in the dark. The truth is that anyone can get HIV/AIDS. HIV/AIDS does not discriminate against any skin color, sex, age, or sexual orientation.

Preventing HIV and AIDS is not very difficult, but only if people are more responsible and take control of their own actions. There is no other way to prevent this disease. Although we may know the facts about HIV/AIDS, it is important not to fall into the belief that it can't happen to us.

COCKTAILS
but Not Happy Hour

Anonymous, 18

KEVIN VUONG

Being HIV positive, it's hard to tell what's worse… dying of AIDS or living with the constraints of my treatment. HIV treatment can be hell. The one I'm on is called HAART (highly active anti-retroviral treatment). I take up to 10 different pills every day and hope that at least 1 of them starts slowing down the virus in my body.

This "cocktail" of prescription drugs might make me live longer, might make me healthier, and might slow down transmission of the virus, but it can't cure me. HIV is a virus that'll always be in my body no matter how many pills I take to fight it.

Treatment is something I have almost no control over. I ALWAYS need my meds with me. At work, at the gym, at school, at home—always. Some meds I take with meals, some before meals, some after meals, some at different times, and so on. I also can't drink or do drugs while I'm on treatment. HAART is hard on my liver, and without a healthy liver, my body can't handle drugs or booze—sometimes I can barely handle food.

The only cocktails I get are the drug cocktails of HAART. It's complicated and expensive, but I hope it's saving my life.

AIDS

Patrick Kabongo

Now this is real talk, you intend to do you in the bed right
You ain't looking left so I hope you damn right
Without warriors you ain't winning a damn fight
But in darkness defense looks damn bright
So you will shine and prevail in protection
But without protection
You could burn in deception
Humiliated bellow all monster
So when you bet you won't catch AIDS without a condom
Someone bit him
When you catch HIV, you'll feel bad for your immune system
Sometimes that's why you have to slow down feelings
Cuz with AIDS you'll slowly breakdown and die from
   its related illness
So pop a tape of HIV in your VHS
And think before you act in transition of sex
Cuz when you let it burn like Usher
Girls they wouldn't want to touch you
It ain't a gay disease
A lot of teenagers and adults could get it
Don't be ignorant to the fact

That this little light thing can make your life go black
So the whole don't use protection, fuck it
Cuz with that scar, alcohol won't help you through it.

This is knowledge poetry and artwork
If you're gonna have sex take a deep thought first
Me, I'm a virgin so y'all can help me and tell me where
    a virgin goes
But that's not the issue
It's all about condoms
They work, but not at all costs especially when you
    break the tissue
But when the blood wants to kiss you
Bye to all the girls cuz they ain't gonna miss you
Guys gonna dis you
So condoms on the penises
Is a serious issue
Well that's all I guess
If you're in that situation put your brain and hormones
    to the test
That would probably be best
Let your brain think and not your dick think
Before he gets hurt all scared with red ink
Knowledge is power
But if you are dirty with the disease don't worry
    about the shower
Cuz your life could go away
Now that you're living by the hour
Protection is good, use it don't be foolish.

Getting TESTED

You can get tested for HIV and other STIs in a number of ways. You can contact your own doctor and ask for the tests, or you can go to a health center or clinic in your community. Some health centers, clinics, and hospitals might offer specific times for HIV and STI testing. HIV clinics may also test for hepatitis B and syphilis but not for gonorrhea or chlamydia. Be sure to check which tests are available in which locations.

Different STIs need different tests. Some—like HIV, hepatitis B, and syphilis—require a simple blood test. Some—like gonorrhea and chlamydia—can be tested through your urine (but in some cases a swab of the infected area might be needed). Others, like crabs, may require a closer inspection of your body.

With some STIs, like HIV, you can get tested anonymously—meaning that you don't have to give your real name. Some STIs, like gonorrhea, need to be reported to a public health agency. The rules for these may be different depending on where you live and where you go, so be sure to ask!

The time it takes to get results will vary depending on the test. If you just need to be inspected for crabs or scabies, the doctor or nurse can examine you and recommend treatment right away. Tests that have to be sent to a lab will take longer. The doctor, nurse, or other clinic staff will let you know how much time it will take. You may have to return at a later date to get the results or you might get the results by phone. In the case of HIV, usually people have to get their results in person. Getting your results in person means that you can ask questions and get more information.

HASSLE-FREE
Clinic

Interview by Asha Blucher

I decided to get tested for HIV. Before I went to my local clinic in Toronto, I wanted to know what testing would be like. So I called the clinic today and asked what I should expect when being tested for HIV/AIDS. This clinic is an approved anonymous testing site for sexual transmitted disease and infections.

Here are some of the questions I asked and the answers I got.

Q. How do I get tested at the clinic?
A. You have to call the clinic to make an appointment.
The wait for an appointment can be up to two weeks.

Q. What is the next step after making the appointment?
A. You would come into the clinic and see a counselor. The counselor will ask a few questions about your sexual habits and help you to better understand risks. The counselor will also talk to you about the test and answer any questions you have about the test for HIV.

Q. What method is used for the testing?
A. A new and safe, sterilized needle is used to withdraw blood from you. The blood will then be sent off to a lab for testing.

Q. How long do I wait for my test results?

A. You would wait approximately 10 days for the results to return.

Q. Would I be notified by phone?

A. No: the clinic does not give results over the phone. You would have to come in person to get your results. This way, the counselor can be there to answer any questions you have. If the results are positive, the counselor can help you determine what support you might need.

Q. What types of testing are available at the clinic?

A. This clinic specializes in anonymous HIV testing, both nominal and non-nominal. These are two methods that clinics use so that we can match your results to you while also keeping your results anonymous and confidential.

Q. What is "nominal" testing?

A. It is a where you give the clinic a name. This could be any name you choose as long as it lets us tell you your results. Whether or not you use your real name, the results will be kept confidential.

Q. What is "non-nominal" testing?

A. Non-nominal testing uses a combination of numbers for identification purposes. Each person tested is assigned a number. The clinic has the list that matches numbers to people, and it is confidential. Anyone else, such as the labs, only sees the numbers.

TAKING CONTROL
Birth Control

CHAPTER 5

Control—You Gotta Have It!

Okay, fellas, so after reading the last chapter, you know all about wrapping your little guy in a condom to protect yourself from HIV/AIDS and all those other nasty STIs. But did you know there's a 3% (or more!) chance a condom won't protect a girl from getting pregnant? WHAT??

If you didn't know that, or you don't know what else you can do to get that 3% down to almost nothing, this chapter is for you. Even if you think you know it, better read on 'cause there's a lot we think we know about birth control that's just plain wrong. Think pulling out before you cum won't get her pregnant? Think again. Ever heard that, if a girl pees right after sex, then she won't get pregnant? Bullshit.

Whether you're playing the field or just exploring sex with one girl, you're responsible for the sperm you leave behind. Sure, we can't get pregnant, but are you ready to be the youngest daddy on your block? So learn the facts and then talk with your lady-friend BEFORE that next hot and steamy moment to save yourselves a lot of stress later on. Damn, there we go again—communication—yo, we can't escape it. Talk to her.

You Thought *What?*
Myths and Facts about
Birth Control

There is a lot of information out there about birth control. Some of it is good and some of it is just plain wrong! You gotta know what's accurate—this ain't no algebra test. Get it wrong and your girl will be failing a pregnancy test!!! You'll kick yourself later if you listen to what a buddy heard from a guy who heard some shit from a reality TV show! Make sure you know where to go to get the accurate info. You don't want to be a daddy before you are ready. You can start right here with this list of common myths and facts about birth control.

Myth: Birth control is the responsibility of the girl because she is the one who can get pregnant.
Fact: Birth control is the responsibility of *both* partners. Simple rule: if it affects her, it affects you. A girl would have to be pregnant for nine months and then give birth, but guys are just as responsible for any new life they helped create! Some guys think they can walk away, but the law sees it differently. If you want your hard-earned dollars for the movies and your Xbox, and not for diapers and baby food (not to mention paying child

support for the next 20 years), you'd better make damn sure that birth control is your responsibility as well.

Myth: The birth control pill is 100% guaranteed and is safe for girls to take.

Fact: Bad news: if you're having sex, there's no birth control method that is 100% guaranteed. But the Pill is among the most effective methods of birth control out there. Don't unzip just yet, bud, 'cause even though birth control pills are pretty effective at preventing pregnancy, they are 0% effective against STIs.

Also, birth control pills are only as reliable as the person who takes them. Your girl has to be crazy organized and reliable. She can't forget to take them, even for one day. And is she on any other pills? Sometimes other meds can screw with how the Pill works in her body. Or how about if she's sick one day and throws up? If it's right after taking her birth control pill, the thing may not have had time to get in gear.

Birth control patches, instead of a pill, can avoid that, but patch or pill, this stuff is messing with your girl's hormones. (That's how it tells her body to not get pregnant.) That can mean increased moodiness, depression, and anxiety. Just what you both want, right?

It's very rare, but birth control pills also increase a girl's risk for getting blood clots, which can do real damage if they get into her brain, lungs, or heart.

Anyway, it's not as simple as her just popping a pill so you can bust a nut. There's serious shit to talk about. Talk to a doctor about anything you and your girl are worried about.

Myth: Condoms are 100% foolproof against pregnancy and STIs.
Fact: I'm telling you again bro, if you're having sex, no birth control method is 100% foolproof. But condoms are *very* damn effective if you use them properly. First of all, you need to make sure that they are not expired and that they haven't been freezing or melting or getting holes poked through them, and then you gotta put one of the things on properly so it doesn't break, tear, or slip off. If you do all that, the condom will protect you from a lot of STIs, but not all. Some live on the skin where a condom doesn't cover. That makes you fair game for infection. (See Chapter 4 for more info.)

Myth: Pulling out before you cum is a good form of birth control.
Fact: Pulling out is NOT a method of birth control. I mean seriously, you really think this is reliable? You really think that, when you're in there and it feels so good and you are about to cum, you're going pull out in time? Even if you think you do have total control, ever heard of pre-cum? That's the liquidy stuff that dribbles out of the tip of your dick when you're turned on but long before you cum. That stuff can contain sperm (not to mention STIs), which can get her pregnant even if you never came!

Myth: Girls can't get pregnant when they are on their period.
Fact: Simple rule: there is always a chance that your girl can get pregnant if your sperm and her vagina are involved. Yeah, there are times when girls are more likely to get pregnant than other times. But do you want to bet a baby on any odds?

Myth: Girls can't get pregnant the first time. Girls can't get pregnant if you have sex standing up. Girls can't get pregnant if you have sex in the tub or shower.

Fact: None of these are true, even if you try them all at once. You know what? If someone starts saying "Girls can't get pregnant if...," then just stop listening. You're better off thinking that girls can *always* get pregnant. That way you will always be thinking about using birth control to *not* get them pregnant.

Myth: I don't need to know about birth control because I am gay.

Fact: Nice try, but everyone should know about birth control. You never know who you'll sex with throughout your life. Many gay guys have sex with a girl at least once. How'd you like be a gay guy who ends up having sex with a girl once and gets her pregnant? Even if you aren't having sex with girls, you should know this stuff. Your straight friends might believe some of these myths—and it'll be up to you to sort them out.

See "Shields Up, Captain!" later in this chapter on pages 198–205 for more info about birth control options.

How She's Built

The Basics of a Woman's Body

In Chapter 1, you got real familiar with your own dangly parts. Well, those parts are only half the equation when it comes to making babies. And if you want to know all about NOT making babies, you'd better know about her parts, too. So here we go.

As you know, the big differences between guys' and girls' bodies become very noticeable during puberty. During puberty in guys, testosterone is the main hormone. In girls, estrogen and progesterone are the main hormones. This stuff tells the cells in a girl's body to start changing. From a science standpoint, her body is setting up shop to start making and caring for babies. That's why, during puberty, a girl's breasts grow (to feed a baby), her hips get wider (to birth a baby), and her period starts (to get rid of the egg that didn't get turned into a baby that month). The actual baby-making parts are all on the inside:

Ovaries

These suckers are the factories where estrogen and progesterone get made. They're also the warehouses for those eggs that are needed to make a baby. These are damn impressive warehouses too—a woman has her entire lifetime supply of eggs stored in there!

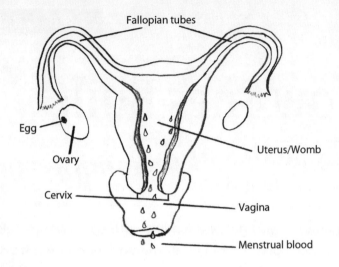

Fallopian tubes

Egg

Ovary

Cervix

Uterus/Womb

Vagina

Menstrual blood

Fallopian Tubes

Sounds like a subway system, and they sort of are. The fallopian tubes are like the train tunnels that the eggs travel through to get to the uterus. After spending all that time in the warehouse (ovary), every month an egg gets to ride a fallopian tube to the uterus for a night on the town with any sperm there to meet it. Sperm is *supposed* to wait at the station (in the uterus), but sometimes it sneaks its way into the fallopian tubes to find an egg early—horny little bastard. That's bad news though, because if that sperm and egg hook up in the tube, that's where a baby will start growing. But the tube just ain't equipped to support a baby. This can be very dangerous for a woman and it's called an ectopic pregnancy, but luckily it's rare.

Uterus

The uterus is where the real action takes place. And by action, we mean pregnancy. The egg comes riding in from the fallopian tubes looking to get it on with some sperm. No sperm there yet? Egg doesn't mind kicking it and settles into the uterus to await the arrival of the sperm. And why not? It's a bad-ass crib for chilling: the walls of the uterus form a thick coating like a sweet cushion. If any sperm comes into the uterus and finds an egg, then crank up the Barry White 'cause it's time for a booty call. The sperm enters the egg and then the egg settles into those cushions... and stays there. A sperm and egg together in that cushiony wall of the uterus means that a girl becomes pregnant. If the sperm is a no-show, the egg won't wait around forever. Egg gathers up all the cushions (the coating of the uterus) and leaves through the vagina. And that's what's happening when a girl gets her period.

Cervix

The cervix is the opening into the vagina from the uterus. Some birth control methods stop sperm from getting in by placing a barrier over the cervix during sex. It's like closing the door so sperm can't get in.

Vagina

The vagina is the opening that leads from the outside of the body to the cervix and on to the uterus. Vaginal sex means having sex by moving the penis in and out of the vagina. The vagina has strong muscles that tighten around a guy's penis. This is what gives guys that enjoyable sensation during sex. And that enjoyable sensation can lead to ejaculation: semen goes squirting into the vagina unless it's trapped inside a condom.

If fallopian tubes are like the subway for eggs, semen is like the bus for sperm. Millions of sperm can ride in just a teaspoon of the stuff. If sperm is released into the vagina, it will travel up to the uterus in search of an egg, like horny guys on Spring Break, heading to Florida in search of hot chicks. The *only* job sperm has is to seek out eggs and join with them to create a baby. Sperm is very good at its job and even sperm released outside and near the vagina can make its way into the uterus!

But the vagina's not just about letting in rowdy sperm. The vagina plays another important role for a woman during sex. When she gets turned on, her vagina produces a slippery liquid that lubricates the vagina. This natural lube allows anything that enters it to slide in easily (like fingers, a penis, or a sex toy). When a woman says she's feeling turned on and getting "wet," this is what she's talking about. When a girl has sex for the first time, the muscles of the vagina are often tight, which can make sex uncomfortable or even painful. Also, if a girl is afraid or nervous, the muscles in the vagina will tighten and make sex difficult. Just because an egg is always waiting for sperm, doesn't mean a girl is always ready for sex!!

The Vulva

No, not the Volvo. The vulva is the whole outer part of a woman's body that leads to the inner reproductive part. When you're talking vulva, you're talking about the vagina and the surrounding area. The vulva is a very sensitive area for a woman 'cause it contains a crazy amount of nerve endings that make sex enjoyable for her. If you want to know what makes girls feel good, you should know your way around the vulva!

Clitoris

Now pay attention! The clitoris (or clit) is a very sensitive, tiny organ that gives girls wicked pleasure during sex. In fact, many women love the feeling they get from the clit more than from their vagina during sex! Rubbing, licking, or sucking the clit can often make a woman cum more than putting your penis or fingers into her vagina—though every girl is different. And check with her before you rub too hard. Just like the head of your dick, the clit contains a whack-load of tiny nerve endings, making it super-sensitive. When a woman gets aroused, the clit fills with blood and gets larger, just like blood fills your dick when it gets hard. The clitoris is located right where the lips meet above the vaginal opening. It's a little bump and often has a hood of skin over it. Ask your girl to give you a tour—you'll both appreciate it!

Labia

This is a fancy word for lips, but not the ones on a girl's face. The labia are the flaps of skin that protect the vagina and clitoris. There are two sets of lips, outer ones and inners ones.

Urethra

Your what now? A urethra is actually a part that both guys and girls have. Basically, it's the tube that piss travels through on its way from the bladder to gettting out of the body. In a girl, it is located between the clitoris and the vagina—it's not part of the vagina. Got it? Girls do not pee from their vagina. In guys, the urethra runs through the penis.

Menstruation

Alright, so now you know all the important she-parts below the equator. It's time to talk about girls' periods. You've made it this far, don't go chickening out now. Sure, knowing how to find the clit is handy, but knowing how menstruation works is more important if you want to avoid being a daddy before you're ready. Just go with the flow here, brother.

Okay, so we all know that, once a girl gets her period for the first time, she can now get pregnant. Here is another quick rundown on what's happening each month:

1. Spin Cycle: A women's body pumps out hormones that set in motion a month-long cycle that ends with a girl getting her period.
2. Egg Man Walking! The cycle gets started when the hormones tell the ovaries to release an egg into the fallopian tube.
3. Wallpapering the Nursery: While the egg is doing its thing traveling along the tube on its way to the uterus, the uterus gets ready by thickening the wall with a cushion of blood and tissue.
4. Eggs Exit: The egg arrives in the uterus and hangs out for a while, but if it doesn't encounter any sperm, it's life cycle ends and the built-up lining of the uterus leaves through the vagina. This is what causes the bleeding when a girl is on her period and it's the last stage of menstruation.

Periods can last anywhere from 2 to 8 days. A lot of girls get extra-special joys with their period—things like cramps, sore breasts, headaches, and feeling weak. Good times. As if that wasn't enough fun, the changing hormone levels can cause mood changes is some girls as well—everything from depression and irritability to just feeling tired. Kinda like first thing in the morning, but all day long. Obvious, this can suck for both the girl and anyone around her. The good news is it doesn't usually last too long.

Some girls can have plenty of warning about their periods 'cause they can practically set their watch by when they get it. But some girls have periods that don't follow a tight schedule. It doesn't come around the same time each month and it is harder to predict. If a girl misses her period, it *may* be a sign that she is pregnant! You better shell out for a home-pregnancy test, or get her to the doctor, if you want to be sure. Yeah, there are other reasons girls can miss their periods, but do you want to take that chance? Hell, a girl can even get what looks and feels like a period even if she is pregnant! So...if you think there is any chance of pregnancy, go get that test done. Now.

Shields Up, Captain! Common Forms of Birth Control

Gordon McLean

You're young. You're hot. You're unstoppable. At least you think so, right? Right.

Think again, buddy! Guys and girls can go through major troubles if they don't protect themselves during sex. You could find yourself sleeping with some girl or some guy and the next month waking up to the news of an STI or a brand new baby boy or girl on the way. Congratulations!

Okay, if you thought your exams were tough, imagine hearing that! We have already talked about how to avoid STIs, but avoiding pregnancy is something we should be aware of as well. As guys, we're part of the team that can make a baby, so we also need to know about birth control. And keep in mind that many of the hormonal based birth controls sometimes have bad effects on women's health and won't EVER protect you from the spread of STIs. You and your partner should do research on birth control. To get you started, here's some crucial info on the most common.

ORAL CONTRACEPTIVE PILL ("THE PILL")

It is one of the most prescribed medications. It is a small pill that women take every day that affects their hormone levels to prevent pregnancy. It is the most reliable form of birth control available, but only if taken properly.

The Pill fools the body into thinking it is already pregnant so the ovaries do not release eggs into the fallopian tubes. You need to trust the girl you are with to be really on top of taking the Pill every day. If you really want to be sure, use a condom. (You should use a condom anyway to protect against STIs.) The Pill can be accessed from a doctor or health clinic and needs a prescription.

Pros

It is very effective if used properly.

There are a lot of choices, so if one brand has strong side effects on your girl, she can try another.

It won't affect a future planned pregnancy. A woman who wants a baby can stop taking the Pill and then will be able to get pregnant.

Cons

It must be taken every day. Even one pill cannot be missed.

It takes a full menstrual cycle (a month or more) after she starts taking the Pill before it becomes effective.

It does not prevent the spread of STIs.

It can cause negative side effects in some women, such as headaches and nausea.

CONDOMS

Condoms are the only form of really hands-on birth control for a guy—and they're the best choice to protect against most STIs. Condoms are available from drug stores. Many clinics and sexual health centers have condoms available as well. Check out youth centers too. Some places will have them available for free.

Pros

They are something guys can use to be an active
    participant in preventing unplanned pregnancy.
They are effective against most STIs.
They are available in many places.
They can be used in the moment.
They are often available free in clinics and youth centers.

Cons

They must be used properly.
They can be damaged, punctured, or worn out.
You or your partner could be allergic to latex,
    although other materials are available.

FEMALE CONDOM

Female condoms are like a large baggy that goes inside the vagina. The penis can slide in and out of the baggy without allowing sperm into the uterus. Female condoms are available from drug stores or health clinics.

Pros

They can be used in the moment.
They can protect against STIs.

Cons

They can be difficult to get.

They can be awkward.

They can be expensive.

Injection (Depo-Provera)

Depo-Provera is a contraceptive that contains the hormone progestin. It is injected into the girl's body and works similar to the Pill—but doesn't need to be taken every day. It stops her ovaries from releasing the monthly egg—so there is nothing to fertilize. It is given to the woman through a needle every 12 weeks. It is really effective in preventing pregnancy. Depo-Provera can be accessed through a doctor or a health clinic.

Pros

Girls don't need to rely on taking a pill every day, but only a shot every 12 weeks.

It is very effective against pregnancy.

It can reduce the number of periods a woman has.

Cons

It must be administered by a health professional.

After about two years, it weakens a woman's bones. This stops when a woman stops taking it.

It can cause weight gain.

It does not protect against STIs.

Contraceptive Patch

This is a patch the girl puts on her abdomen, butt, upper arm, or upper torso. It releases estrogen and progestin, which prevent ovulation, which then prevents pregnancy. It works the same as the Pill, but it is in patch form. She wears a new patch every week for three weeks of each month. In the fourth week, when she doesn't wear the patch, she gets her period.

Pros
It doesn't need to be taken every day.
It is very effective against pregnancy.

Cons
It is possible the patch will irritate the skin—
causing itching, burning, or a rash.
The patch could possibly come loose and fall off.
It does not protect against STIs.

NUVA RING

This is a soft flexible ring worn in the vagina for three weeks of the month. It contains estrogen and progestin, which are absorbed continuously, directly into the bloodstream through the vaginal wall. The hormones prevent ovulation, so prevent pregnancy. A girl puts the ring in herself and takes it out on the last week of the month, when she gets her period.

Pros
It doesn't need to be taken every day,
just put in once per month.
It doesn't interfere with sex.

Cons
It may cause discomfort in the vagina
(bleeding, itching, burning).
It may fall out although this is uncommon.
It does not protect against STIs.

OTHER OPTIONS

There are other birth control options but they are not very common, especially for young people. Some of them are too unreliable, some may cause harm, and some are used by people who are older and are no longer planning to have (or have any more) children.

Diaphragm

This is a latex cap that covers the opening to the cervix and prevents sperm from swimming inside. Women have to have diaphragms sized by a doctor to ensure a tight seal. Like a condom, it can be used immediately to prevent pregnancy but it is not that common anymore. It does not prevent against all STIs. One advantage is that it doesn't require hormones.

IUD

IUD stands for Intrauterine Device. Basically it is a device that is inserted into the uterus. It is a copper wire in a T shape and it interferes with sperm in the uterus. A doctor must size and insert IUDs. While effective, they can cause cramping and irritation, and they may come out. As with other forms of birth control except condoms, they do not protect against STIs.

IUS (Mirena)

IUS stands for Intrauterine System. It is also a device that a doctor inserts into the uterus. Just like an IUD, the IUS is a T shape, but instead of the copper wire that an IUD uses to interfere with sperm, an IUS has a cylinder that contains the hormone levonorgestrel. This cylinder slowly releases the hormone, which affects the uterus in a way that makes it difficult for sperm to enter and prevents an egg from settling into the lining. The IUS is effective but can also come out accidentally and needs to be replaced every five years. It also offers no protection at all against STIs.

Spermicide

This is a chemical in the form of a cream, gel, foam, or film used to reduce the risk of unplanned pregnancy by killing off the sperm that you ejaculate. Some women have severe allergies to spermicides. Spermicides irritate the mouth, vagina, and anus, which increases your chances of getting an STI. Spermicides, such as nonoxynol-9, can having a numbing effect as well.

Sponge

A sponge contains spermicide and is inserted into the vagina. It acts as a barrier and kills sperm. Sponges left in the vagina for too long can cause serious health problems. Because sponges use spermicide, there could be allergy issues or irritation.

Cervical Cap

This is a deep latex cap that fits against the cervix and prevents sperm and bacteria from entering the cervix. Much like the diaphragm, it must be sized by a doctor. The cervical cap may get knocked out of place during sex, so many woman prefer another form a birth control. It doesn't protect against some STIs.

Vasectomy

This is surgery that blocks a guy's sperm duct and prevents sperm from entering the semen. This will prevent men from becoming parents in the future, so it is not a good choice for young people. Older men who have had children already or who know they never will may choose this option. However, it doesn't protect against STIs. This is a quick surgery that can be done at the doctor's office.

Tubal Ligation

This is a more serious surgery than a vasectomy and is done on the woman. The fallopian tubes are pinched, cut, or blocked from letting eggs pass into the uterus. This surgery is permanent and is very difficult to reverse. This option is most often chosen by woman who are done having children.

Monthly Charting

Some women will keep track of their menstrual cycles (their periods) so that they can estimate when or when not to participate in unprotected sex. However, this is not always accurate and does not protect against STIs. This method takes time, can be very complicated, involves record-keeping and temperature-taking, and can be difficult for woman with periods that aren't regular.

LEARN MORE

It is important to learn all you can about birth control options and pick the one that is best for your partner and yourself. Since it takes both egg and sperm to make a baby, BOTH people involved are responsible for making sure that protection is in place. Even if your girlfriend misses a Pill and doesn't tell you, the baby is still your baby, so make sure you and your partner talk about birth control.

Remember the only way to prevent pregnancy 100% is to avoid having sex that places sperm near or in the vagina.

WRAPPED
SAUSAGES
A Guide to Putting on a Condom

Here are some more tips on using condoms. Also check out "Condoms at the Minimum" on pages 140–142. You can never know this stuff too well—condoms only work when they are used properly! When condoms *don't* work, it's usually not because there is something wrong with the condom, but because it was not used properly.

So guys, make sure you know how to use one. Practice if you have to. You don't want to be fumbling around in that moment, and you sure as hell don't want any accidents.

Here are some DOs and DON'Ts around condoms:
- DO keep condoms in a cool dry place—not hot and not freezing. DON'T ever keep them in your wallet or back pocket. DO protect them from heat, sharp objects, and wear and tear. DO keep them in a box in your backpack or bag—some places even give out plastic condom holders that keep them safe.
- DO always check the expiry date on the package. Expired condoms can be defective. They may be latex but they don't last forever.

- DO use the right size of condom for you. DON'T buy extra large just to show off. Regular fits most people: a regular-sized condom can fit over your ENTIRE ARM! Every guy wants to think he needs the large size but you don't. If your condom is too big, it won't stay in place and can tear more easily. What's more embarassing: using a regular-sized condom or having a large one slip off?
- DO only use a water-based lubricant if you are going to use extra lube. DON'T use lubricants with petroleum and other chemical ingredients because they can break down the latex and tear the condom.
- DON'T use more than one condom. You may think, "Hey, if one condom is safe, two must be safer!" WRONG! Doubling up on condoms can lead to problems. One condom used properly should do the trick.
- DO only use a condom once. DON'T ever reuse a condom.
- DO practice, practice, practice. Practice putting a condom on yourself or on a banana or a cucumber. If you know what you are doing, slipping on a condom before sex can be quick and easy and not break up your "moment."

Okay, so how do you use a condom properly? No problem, follow these simple instructions. Repeat them until you know them well.

1. Have condoms with you. If you don't have any condoms, don't have sex. Don't take any chances.
2. Check the expiry date to make sure the condom is still safe to use.
3. Check the package for punctures or damage. If there is air in the package, there are no punctures.

4. Push the condom into one corner of the package and tear the package open from the other side.

5. Squeeze the tip of the condom and place it on the head of your penis. You want to be sure there is space at the tip to catch the semen when you cum. If you don't leave any space, the condom may burst.

6. Unroll the condom all the way to the base of your penis.

7. When you are finished having sex, hold the base of the condom as you pull your penis out.

8. Away from your partner, slip the condom off, tie it off so the contents can't leak, and throw it away.

"NO REGRETS" MY ASS!
The Emergency Contraception Pill

Sometimes things don't go as planned. Maybe the condom broke or slipped off. Maybe you had sex when you were drunk or high, and you didn't use a condom. Or maybe you just got caught up in the moment and went in unprotected. Whatever the reason, you may have started yourself down the road to fatherhood without meaning to.

So, you're thinking to yourself, "Uh oh, that was probably not such a good idea." What do you do about it? Well, lucky for you there is an option for those moments when your judgment was not so good or an accident happens. It's called the Emergency Contraceptive Pill, or ECP. To prevent pregnancy, ECP can be taken by your female partner within 72 hours of unprotected sex.

What is ECP?
The Emergency Contraceptive Pill is actually two pills. The pills have hormones in them like the ones in the birth control pill. If taken within 72 hours of unprotected sex, those hormones can reduce the chances of pregnancy.

When should ECP be used?

You should not consider ECP as a regular form of birth control. It should be used for emergencies only. ECP should be taken for the following situations:

- You had unprotected sex with a girl.
- You tried to "pull out" but didn't.
- The condom broke or slipped off.
- Your sperm, for whatever reason, came in contact with any area around your partner's vagina.
- Your partner forgot to take her birth control pills, is taking medication that makes the Pill not work right, or has thrown up within an hour of taking the Pill.
- She was forced to have sex, was sexually assaulted, or was abused.

Does ECP work?

If taken within 72 hours, ECP *can* reduce the chance of pregnancy BUT there are no guarantees. Depending on the kind of ECP taken, chances of getting pregnant can be reduced by 75%–85%. This still leaves a 15%–25% chance that pregnancy will occur. To be safer, it is best to use a reliable form of birth control and avoid needing to use ECP. If your partner is already pregnant, from previous sex or if more than 72 hours has passed, ECP will NOT make the pregnancy go away. ECP is not an abortion pill.

How will ECP affect my partner?

The most common side effect of ECP is feeling sick and throwing up. Some doctors give a woman something to take in order to prevent that. If your partner throws up within one hour of taking ECP, she will have to take it again. Other side effects may be sore breasts, headache, and bloating.

How do we get ECP?

You don't need to have a prescription to get ECP, but you will have to ask for it. You can get it by visiting your doctor, a health clinic, or the hospital emergency department. You can also get it from a drug store, but it is behind the counter so you will have to ask the pharmacist to get it for you. Prices can vary from place to place so you can call around to find the cheapest. Don't hesitate—the faster you can get ECP, the better.

How will we know if it worked?

If you partner gets her period within three weeks of taking ECP, she should be safe. However, if she doesn't get her period, you are going to need to take a pregnancy test. ECP can cause irregular bleeding so her period may not come when expected. Remember that ECP is not as effective as condoms, the Pill, and other forms of birth control.

OPTING *for* OPTIONS
Abortion, Adoption, and Parenting

She's pregnant. For whatever reason, your sperm and her egg got together, and now a baby is on the way. You and you partner now have some tough decisions to make. Are you ready to have a baby? Can you support a child? Do you even want one? Here is some information about your three main choices:

ABORTION

One of the options available to people in Canada and the U.S. is abortion. Now, there are lots of opinions out there about abortion. Don't let that get to you. Find out about the facts, think about how *you* feel, and talk to your partner. When it comes right down to it, it is your partner's decision, but she could use all the support you can give her. It is her body that will be affected. You may really want to try and have the baby, but if that's not the decision she makes, you need to respect that.

So what happens if you and your girl choose to have an abortion? Both of you should see her doctor or go to a health clinic and talk about it. If you or your partner is having a hard time dealing with the abortion, there are people you can talk to. The doctor will then refer you to a clinic or hospital for the abortion. In Canada, abortions are covered under public health plans so it shouldn't cost you anything, but not all hospitals perform abortions and not all provinces have clinics. In the United States, the average cost is around $375, but it can be lower or higher.

Once an appointment has been set up, a doctor will use suction to remove the contents of the uterus. This will end the pregnancy. Most abortions will only be performed in the first trimester, which is the first three months of pregnancy. After that, you will have to look at other options. If, after having an abortion, your partner is still having a hard time dealing with the decision (or you are), talk to someone. Women who have an abortion will still be able to get pregnant later when and if they decide they are ready.

Abortion is not a form of birth control. It should be done only when other birth control options have failed and it is too late for the Emergency Contraception Pill. Even if you decide that having an abortion is the best decision for you, it can still be a hard choice to make and comes with a lot of emotion. If your partner chooses to have an abortion, it isn't because she doesn't love or trust you. She just isn't ready to have a kid— yours or anyone else's.

See the Resources section at the back of the book for suggestions on where to find more information about abortion options in your area.

ADOPTION

If your partner doesn't believe that abortion is the best option for her, but doesn't want to raise a baby, adoption is always an option. There are many couples and families out there that can give a baby a good home. There are many people who really want a child but are unable to have one. The choice of adoption can bring great joy to someone else's life, but it can also be difficult. It can be hard to give up a child, especially when you see him or her for the first time. For some people, knowing that they have a kid out there, somewhere is hard.

If you and your partner do agree to give the baby up for adoption, your first step is to talk to your doctor or health clinic. They will get you in touch with someone who can give you all the facts and talk to you about the adoption process in your area. Adoption procedures are a little different in every province and state, but in general, you will have the option to choose either an open adoption or a closed adoption.

An **open adoption** means that you and your partner let the adoptive parents know your identity. You may even choose to stay in touch as the child grows up. It all depends on how involved you want to be and how comfortable you and the adoptive parents are with each other. If you share your identity and communicate with the adoptive parents, but you don't meet them face-to-face, it is considered a **semi-open adoption**.

A **closed adoption** means that your identity is kept confidential, and you won't know the identities of the adoptive parents. You may each learn basic family and medical information about each other, but your names and locations will not be shared.

Adoptions can be arranged privately by individuals (like if an aunt and uncle or friends of the family want to adopt your baby), by private adoption agencies, or by public government agencies. In every case, the people involved must abide by the same adoption laws. Whenever there are expenses to be paid, they are usually paid by the adoptive parents, not by the birth parents. If you choose adoption, know that there are many low- and no-cost options available to you.

See the Resources section at the back of the book for suggestions on where to find more information about adoption options in your area.

PARENTING

Deciding to become a parent is a huge deal. Looking after a child takes a lot of work, a lot of money, a lot of time, and a lot of patience. In fact, if you do become a dad, it will be the most important responsibility you will ever have. After all a baby is a human being who needs food, clothing, shelter, and emotional nurturing—not to mention health care and education. On the other hand, all that work can be worth it because knowing and parenting this human being could give you the most amazing experiences that you ever have.

If your partner decides she is going to keep the baby and raise the kid, you need to be honest with her and with yourself about how involved you are willing to be. There are a lot of things to consider. Will you stay in school? Will you work? How much time will you be available to look after the baby? What will you do if you have to choose between hanging out with your friends and looking after the baby? Will you and your partner stay together as a couple? Will you live together? Do you have family and friends who can support you emotionally? Are you aware of your legal and financial responsibilities as the father? Be sure to talk about all of these issues with your partner before the baby is born. Try to be realistic about your expectations.

The good news is that you are not alone. Start with a doctor. It is very important that your partner

- see a doctor as soon as she knows she is pregnant and
- immediately stop smoking, drinking alcohol, or using drugs as these things can interfere with the development of the baby

The doctor can help prepare your partner for a healthy pregnancy, including recommending vitamins and exercises and keeping track of both your partner's and the baby's health over the coming months. Since pregnancy happens to your partner's body, not to yours, it's important that you be supportive and encouraging about her efforts to stay healthy, but let her make the decisions.

There are many organizations out there that offer support for teenage parents. These groups can offer

- knowledgeable and supportive people to talk with
- programs and classes to help you prepare for what's next in the pregnancy, for birthing, and for parenting
- an opportunity to meet other young parents going through the same experiences as you

Ask your doctor or health clinic to recommend groups in your area.

See the Resources section at the back of the book for suggestions on where to find more information about being a teen parent.

I Guess My Buddies Can Swim After All

Anonymous, 20

Okay, so it all started one August when I met a local girl in an online chat room. Even though all the previous girls I talked to on that site were just another contact on my MSN Messenger list, there was something different about this girl. Instead of just flirting, we talked about our goals and what we wanted in life, and we really shared what we had going on inside our hearts. It's like she was made for me, and what's more amazing is that she seemed to be falling in love with me as well! Perfect! Just knowing her made me change my life around. I stayed out of trouble with the law and away from weed and any other drugs.

Well, after about two weeks of chatting online, we made plans to meet. Even though I've always thought the "beautiful inside" speech is just a load of shit to cover up for someone's ugly exterior, I actually like the fact we met first online. It's better because we liked each other for who we were and not what we looked like. And when we met in person, she was beautiful, but I was attracted to her even more because of everything we'd talked about.

Two weeks later, we were completely in love. One night, we were making out and touching hardcore, and we couldn't take it anymore. We went into the bedroom, took each other's clothes off, and had sex. I had condoms in my pocket but I didn't use them. I really didn't want to use a condom 'cause this was our first time and I wanted it to feel amazing. It was amazing.

A few months went by and we continued to have sex often, always without condoms. She wasn't getting pregnant, so I just thought my sperm was dead from my drug days. More months went by and it was all good. We had fun and enjoyed life, did everything together, and pregnancy was never on our minds. Then one day, seven months later, she started feeling sick. She would get nauseous and dizzy and have mood swings and weird food cravings—all the usual signs of pregnancy.

We made an appointment for a pregnancy test at a local clinic. Obviously, we wanted to know as soon as possible so we could have time to review our options. The day came and she had the test done, and 10 minutes later the nurse brought us the results: she was pregnant.

I was shocked, but not really afraid—not like those people who get all suicidal and think life is over just 'cause they're pregnant. Sure, it kind of worried me to think about living our best years tied down with a kid. And going through with an abortion didn't sound like fun. But I really loved her and the fact she had my kid inside her was a nice thought, and I now knew my sperm was working just fine. We both took some time and gave our situation a lot of thought. We would have loved to keep the baby, but we decided it would be better to wait a few years until we were economically stable and were more prepared overall for a kid. We decided that she would have an abortion.

We made the appointment. As we waited for the day to come, she had mood swings and it was like she was a different person at times. But I loved her so I comforted her and was always there for her, even when she was in the worst of moods.

I also spoke to my favorite teacher about the whole thing. He's the best teacher I've ever had, and I can talk about anything with the guy. He couldn't understand how I didn't want to get her pregnant yet I wasn't using condoms or other birth control. I couldn't explain it, really. I guess, like I said it, it feels too good without a condom and I thought my sperm was dead anyway. I guess I just got lucky for a while.

Then the day came and it was time for the abortion. We went back to the clinic where they did some tests before we went to the actual hospital. This all began early in the morning and I waited in the hospital for hours until the procedure was done. Afterward, she was under close supervision for about an hour after waking up from the anesthetic. The doctor said the abortion had gone perfectly and she would be fine. I was relieved to hear that 'cause the whole time she was in there I was worried about what could happen and that it might be painful. It was weird because, when she came out from it, she was normal and smiling; she even looked relieved. I had expected her to come out limping in pain or something. I was relieved as well to see her smiling and to know she was no longer pregnant. The doctor said she shouldn't do any exercise, drink alcohol, or have sex for two weeks from that day. Besides that she was fine and could still go to school.

This whole experience has taught me to use birth control, like we do now, and to give things more thought before I do them, to think of the long-term consequences of my actions. We're still together and she doesn't seem traumatized or anything from the experience. The only thing is that we really wanted to keep the baby. It would have been nice if we could have, but I guess it's something we can look forward to in the future.

The Day I Became a Father

Anonymous, 19

I became a father last August. It was the December before that my girlfriend told me she had missed her period. She also said her cycle was sometimes like that, so at first I didn't think anything of it. But she started this job the next day and she threw up on her new boss! Then I started to ask myself "what if...?" but I still didn't think it was true.

The next day, we bought a home pregnancy test and the results were positive. When she told me, I told her she should go to the walk-in clinic and see a doctor to be sure. She did and when she came back she had a bunch of pamphlets and told me the results came back positive again. I was going to be a father.

That's when I got scared but excited at the same time. We both knew we wanted to keep the baby. I thought to myself, what are the next nine months going to be like? What will our lives be like after the baby is born? Somehow, it still didn't feel real. And then we went for our first ultrasound. When I saw this almost microscopic view of my baby, I was overwhelmed. The heartbeat was so strong. I felt so proud.

Months went by and my girlfriend felt sick a lot. Every night, I would read and speak to her belly. Around four months into the pregnancy, we found out we were having a baby boy. I was like, "Yup that's all me. I did that." My girlfriend had the second ultrasound when I was at work so she went with her mom. They said they could see him so clearly and I was upset. How could I miss that? I promised myself that I wouldn't miss the next ultrasound for the world.

The next ultrasound was the last one before the baby was born. That tiny dot from the first ultrasound had grown into a baby, and I saw my son open and close his fist in her stomach. It was weird but interesting to see a life develop from something so small.

Then came the day. It was 9:45 in the morning when my girl said she saw some blood in her pee. We went to the hospital and after 16 hours of labor, my son was born. He weighed 3.71 kilograms (8 pounds and 3 ounces). It was the best day of my life.

At first, becoming a father felt real scary. I didn't know if I was cut out for all the drama in the nighttime or diapers and all that stuff. I couldn't even handle the fact of him coming out of my girl. Honestly, it was a very disgusting process and a lot of work. And that was just the birth. Once we brought him home, I thought: this is going to be a lot of work. Am I going to be like my father and eventually leave him like my father left me? I had real problems growing up, getting involved in bad shit, and even getting in trouble with police. All that stuff could've been avoided if my dad was there to help us out. I knew I didn't want my son to go through what I went through. I want him to have someone to talk to about growing up, friends, and eventually sex. There are just some things that a man can't talk to his mom about.

Dads act like they don't play an important part, but we do. When at first we took my son home, I was real nervous. I was thinking things like, Am I going to drop him? Will he love me the same as his mom or at all? But then I started noticing that, when I spent time with him, he wanted me as well. Then I realized that, if you ain't there, how is your child going to know you at all? I still read books to him, play music to him, and even sing to him. It may sound corny but it is the best feeling in the world, being a dad. He's my little man and I love him. Who needs the partying when you got your seed? It's something money can't buy.

We hope you find the following numbers and websites helpful. However, they are not meant to replace professional advice. Their inclusion does not constitute an endorsement by the authors or the publisher. Please also keep in mind that phone numbers and website addresses and content are subject to change.

Kids Help Phone – **www.kidshelpphone.ca** – 1-800-668-6868 (CANADA)
Kids' Helpline – **www.kidscrisis.com** – 1-877-KIDS-400 (UNITED STATES)

Chapter 1 – Love Machine: The Penis
Afraid to Ask – **www.afraidtoask.com**
American Social Health Association (ASHA): I Wanna Know: Puberty –
    www.iwannaknow.org/puberty/index.html
Cool Nurse: Men's Health Center – **www.coolnurse.com/male_health.htm**
RU Thinking About Sex and Relationships: The Lad Pad –
    www.ruthinking.co.uk/lad-delay/new-body-new-man.aspx
Scarleteen: Sex Ed for the Real World: Boyfriend! –
    www.scarleteen.com/article/boyfriend
Spider Bytes: A New Spin on Sexual Health for Teens –
    www.spiderbytes.ca/Puberty/Puberty.shtml (puberty)
TeensHealth – **www.kidshealth.org/teen/**

Chapter 2 – Making the Connection: Relationships
Healthy Relationships:
Advocates for Youth – **www.advocatesforyouth.org**
Go Ask Alice! – **www.goaskalice.columbia.edu**
Sexuality and U – **http://sexualityandu.ca/teens/what-4.aspx**
Teenwire.com – **www.teenwire.com**
Youth Embassy – **www.youthembassy.com**
Youthwork – **www.youthwork.com/youthinfo.html**

Lesbian, Gay, Bisexual, Transgender, Transexual, Two-Spirited, Intersex, Queer and Questioning Relationships:
AlterHéros – **www.alterheros.com/english/youth/**
Nova Scotia Youth Project – **www.youthproject.ns.ca**
PFLAG (Parents, Families and Friends of Lesbians and Gays) – **www.pflag.org**
PFLAG Canada – **www.pflagcanada.ca**
Youth Resource – **http://www.youthresource.com**

Transgender Info:
Transproud – www.transproud.com
Youth Resource – www.youthresource.com (search "transgender")

Homophobia/Transphobia/Biphobia/Heterosexism:
Advocates for Youth – www.advocatesforyouth.org/lessonplans/activistally1.htm
   (fighting homophobia and transphobia)
Alterhéros – www.alterheros.com
Canadian Rainbow Health Coalition – www.rainbowhealth.ca/english/
   homophobia.html (homophobia and heterosexism)
Gay-Straight Alliance Network – www.gsanetwork.org/resources/straight.html
   (straight allies)
Trans Accessibility Project – www.queensu.ca/humanrights/tap/
   3discrimination.htm (fighting transphobia and discrimination)

Abuse:
Love Doesn't Have to Hurt Teens – www.apa.org/pi/cyf/teen.pdf
Love Is Not Abuse – www.loveisnotabuse.com
Men Can Stop Rape – www.mencanstoprape.org
Men for Change – www.chebucto.ns.ca/CommunitySupport/
   Men4Change/what.html
National Youth Violence Prevention Resource Center: Teen Dating Violence
   – www.safeyouth.org/scripts/topics/dateviolence.asp
The Network Against Abuse in Same-Sex Relationships –
   www.bcifv.org/resources/samesex.shtml
Teen Relationships – www.teenrelationships.org

Chapter 3 – Let's Get It On: Sex
General:
Afraid to Ask – www.afraidtoask.com
BirdsAndBees.org – www.birdsandbees.org
Canadian Federation for Sexual Health (formerly Planned Parenthood Federation
   of Canada) – www.cfsh.ca
The Coalition for Positive Sexuality – www.positive.org
The Coalition for Positive Sexuality: Just Say Yes Campaign –
   www.positive.org/JustSayYes
Guttmacher Institute – www.guttmacher.org (statistics, fact sheets)
It's Your (Sex) Life – www.mtv.com/thinkmtv/features/
   sexual_health/iysl_guide/index1.jhtml
Options for Sexual Health (OPT) – www.optionsforsexualhealth.org
Planned Parenthood Federation of America – www.plannedparenthood.org

RU thinking about sex and relationships – **www.ruthinking.co.uk/**
Scarleteen: Sex Ed for the Real World: Boyfriend! –
  www.scarleteen.com/article/boyfriend
Sex, Etc.: Sexual Ed by Teens for Teens! – **www.sxetc.org**
Sexuality and U – **www.sexualityandu.ca**
SpiderBytes: A New Spin on Sexual Health for Teens – **www.spiderbytes.ca**
TeensHealth – **www.kidshealth.org/teen/**
Think Again Campaign – **www.thinkagain.ca**
Toronto, City of, Public Health: Sexual Health Information –
  www.toronto.ca/health/sexualhealth/index.htm

Lesbian, Gay, Bisexual, Transgender, Transexual, Two-Spirited, Intersex, Queer and Questioning:
GLBT (Gay, Lesbian, Bisexual & Transgender) National Youth Talkline –
  http://www.glnh.org/talkline/index.html
  1-800-246-7743 (US only)
Lesbian Gay Bi Trans Youth Line – **www.youthline.ca**
National Youth Advocacy Coalition – **www.nyacyouth.org** (LGBTQ Youth)
Nova Scotia Youth Project – **www.youthproject.ns.ca**

People with Disabilities:
Canadian Federation for Sexual Health: Sexuality and Disability –
  www.cfsh.ca/Sexual_Health_Info/Sexuality-and-Disability/
Disability Online: Disability and Sexual Issues –
  http://www.disability.vic.gov.au/dsonline/dsarticles.nsf/pages/
  Disability_and_sexual_issues?OpenDocument
MossRehab ResourceNet: Sexuality and Disability Fact Sheet –
  www.mossresourcenet.org/sexuali.htm
Queers on Wheels – **www.queersonwheels.com** (LGBTQ with physical disabilities)

People of Colour:
Advocates for Youth: Info and Support for Youth of Color –
  www.advocatesforyouth.org/youth/info/yoc.htm
Ambiente Joven – **www.ambientejoven.org** (sexuality resource for LGBTQ
  youth in Spanish)
Youth Resource – **www.youthresource.com/living/yoc/index.htm**

Age of Consent:
Avert – **www.avert.org/aofconsent.htm**
Cool Nurse: Age of Consensual Sex (US) –
  http://www.coolnurse.com/consent.htm

Legal Information Society of Nova Scotia: Age of Consent to Sex Goes Up (Canada) –
www.legalinfo.org/index.php?option=com_content&task=
view&id=179&Itemid=10

Sexual Violence:
1in6.org – **www.1in6.org/index.html** (for young men who have faced
unwanted or abusive sexual experiences)
Men Can Stop Rape – **www.mencanstoprape.org**
Men for Change –
www.chebucto.ns.ca/CommunitySupport/Men4Change/what.html
Men: Preventing Date Rape – **http://ub-counseling.buffalo.edu/coercion.shtml**
New York City Alliance Against Sexual Assault –
www.nycagainstrape.org/survivors_factsheet_60.html
Project Respect – **www.yesmeansyes.com/**
RAINN (Rape, Abuse & Incest National Network) – 1-800-656-HOPE (US only)
www.rainn.org
Scarborough Hospital Sexual Assault Care Centre – **www.sacc.to/**
Surviving to Thriving: Healing and Hope for Survivors of Sexual Violence –
www.survivingtothriving.org/factsandmyths

**Chapter 4 – The Thin Red Line: HIV/AIDS and Other Sexually
Transmitted Infections**
General:
Adolescent AIDS Program – **www.adolescentaids.org/**
American Social Health Association (ASHA) – **www.iwannaknow.org**
ASHA STI Resource Center Hotline 1-800-227-8922
Aware Foundation: Emergency Health Resources – **www.awarefounda
tion.org/resources/std_hotlines.aspx** (STI and AIDS hotline listings)
BirdsAndBees.org – **www.birdsandbees.org**
Centers for Disease Control and Prevention – **www.cdc.gov**
Centers for Disease Control and Prevention: National Prevention Information
Network (CDC NPIN): HIV/AIDS, STD, or TB prevention
1-800-458-5231 (US only)
1-404-679-3860 (International)
Health Canada: Sexually Transmitted Infections – **www.hc-sc.gc.ca/dc-ma/
sti-its/index_e.html**
Peer to Peer website: Stop, Think, Be Safe! – **www.stopthinkbesafe.org**
(STD prevention)
Public Health Agency of Canada: Sexually Transmitted Infections –
www.phac-aspc.gc.ca/publicat/std-mts/index-eng.html
Sex Etc.: Sex in the States – **www.sexetc.org/state** (health clinics by state)

HIV/AIDS:

AIDS Committee of Toronto – **www.actoronto.org**
AIDS and Sexual Health Hotline – 1-800-668-2437, 1-416-392-2437 (Canada)
AIDS*info* Information Service – **www.aidsinfo.nih.gov/**
    1-800-448-0440 (US only)
    1-301-519-0459 (International)
    1-888-480-3739 (TTY/TDD)
Asian Community AIDS Services – **www.acas.org**
Avert – **www.avert.org**
Be Real – **www.ru4real.ca/** (HIV/AIDS and sexual health information for gay
    and bisexual men and other men who have sex with men)
The Body – **www.thebody.com** (extensive AIDS/HIV site)
Canadian Aboriginal AIDS Network – **www.caan.ca**
Centers for Disease Control and Prevention – **www.cdc.gov/hiv**
Health Canada – **www.hc-sc.gc.ca/dc-ma/aids-sida/index_e.html**
Motherisk – **www.motherisk.org/women/hiv.jsp** (HIV treatment in pregnancy)
National AIDS Hotline (US only) 1-800-232-4636 (in English and Spanish)
    1-888-232-6348 Deaf Access (TTY)
National HIV and STD Testing Resources – **www.hivtest.org/**
National Minority AIDS Council – **www.nmac.org**
The National Native American AIDS Prevention Center (NNAAPC) –
    www.nnaapc.org

Safer Sex:

AIDS Committee Toronto – **www.actoronto.org/website/home.nsf/**
    pages/mysexlife
Public Health Agency of Canada – **www.phac-aspc.gc.ca/publicat/**
    epiu-aepi/std-mts/condom_e.html
Youth Resource: Safer Sex: Partner Communication
    www.youthresource.com/safersex/communication.htm

Chapter 5 – Taking Control: Birth Control
General:

Association of Reproductive Health Professionals (ARHP) – **www.arhp.org/**
    patienteducation/interactivetools/choosing/index.cfm?ID=275
    (interactive quiz to find a method of birth control right for your partner and you)
BirdsAndBees.org – **www.birdsandbees.org**
Cool Nurse: Birth Control Myths – **www.coolnurse.com/bcmyths.htm**
Health Canada: Birth Control – **www.hc-sc.gc.ca/hl-vs/sex/control/index_e.html**
The Red Spot – **www.onewoman.com/redspot** (women's biology, periods)

Sexuality and U – **http://sexualityandu.ca/teens/contraception.aspx**
(contraception)
Stay Teen.Org – **www.stayteen.org**

Emergency Contraception:
Ann Rose's Ultimate Birth Control – **www.ultimatebirthcontrol.com**
Back Up Your Birth Control with Emergency Contraception –
www.backupyourbirthcontrol.org
The Emergency Contraception Website – **www.NOT-2-LATE.com**

Abortion:
Abortion Clinics On-line – **www.gynpages.com** (US and International clinics)
After Abortion – **http://afterabortion.com/men_relatives.html**
(help for men, relatives, and friends of a woman who's had an abortion)
Choice USA – **www.choiceusa.org/documents/myths.pdf**
Exhale – **www.4exhale.org**
After-abortion counseling helpline 1-866-439–4253 (English, Spanish,
Cantonese, Mandarin, Tagalog, and Vietnamese-speaking counselors available)
Feminist Women's Health Center: Abortion Information – **www.fwhc.org/abortion**
Indigenous Women's Reproductive Rights and Pro-Choice Page –
www.nativeshop.org/pro-choice.html
NARAL – National Abortion and Reproductive Rights Action League –
www.naral.org (pro-choice)
National Abortion Federation – **www.prochoice.org**
Hotline – 1-800-772-9100 (both Canada and US)
Sex Etc.: Sex in the States – **www.sexetc.org/state** (listings of rights to abortion
in each state)
Scarleteen – **www.scarleteen.com/article/advice/crisis_pregnancy_**
centers_harm_not_help (about pregnancy crisis centers)

Teen Pregnancy, Adoption, and Parenthood:
Adoption.com: Are You Ready to Parent? – **www.parentingvsadoption.com**
Adoption.com: Birthmother Resources – **www.birthmother.com** (for those
considering placing a child for adoption (pre-placement) and those who have
placed (post-placement))
Adoption.com: Expectant Fathers – **www.crisispregnancy.com/**
birth-mother/expectant-fathers.html
Adoption.com: Teen Pregnancy – **www.teenpregnancy.com**
American Pregnancy Association – **www.americanpregnancy.org**
American Pregnancy Association: Paternity Testing –
www.americanpregnancy.org/prenataltesting/paternitytesting.html

American Pregnancy Helpline: Guy's Corner – **www.thehelpline.org/guys-corner/**
Motherisk – **www.motherisk.org/women/index.jsp** (substance abuse and
   medical conditions during pregnancy)
   1-877-327-4636 – Alcohol and Substance
   1-888-246-5840 – HIV and HIV Treatment
National Advocates for Pregnant Women –
   www.advocatesforpregnantwomen.org
StorkNet – **www.storknet.com**
TeenParents.org – **www.teenparents.org**

Other Cool Links:
Aboriginal Youth Network – **www.ayn.ca**
AboutHealth: Talking Kid to Kid – **www.abouthealth.com/t_talking.htm**
AdiosBarbie.com – **http://www.adiosbarbie.com/features/features_godsey.html**
   (body image)
Canadian Youth for Choice – **http://www.cyouthc.ca/** (policy-making)
Colage – **www.colage.org** (movement of children, youth, and adults with one
   or more lesbian, gay, bisexual, transgender and/or queer (LGBTQ) parents)
The Deaf Queer Resource Center (DQRC) – **www.deafqueer.org**
Guttmacher Institute – **www.guttmacher.org** (fact sheets and statistics) (USA)
NOAH: New York Online Access to Health – **www.noah-health.org/**
   (wide range of information, in English and Spanish)
Spank Mag! Youth Culture Defined by Youth – **www.spankmag.com**
   (forums related to sexuality and relationships)
Statistics Canada – **www.statcan.ca** (statistics about abortion, teen pregnancy, etc.)
Youth Action Network – **www.youthactionnetwork.org** (youth activism)

GLOSSARY

abortion – A medical procedure to remove the embryo or fetus from the uterus. Performed when a woman decides to end her pregnancy.

abstinence – To abstain from sex – meaning to not have sex

AIDS – acquired immune deficiency syndrome: a medical condition caused by HIV that destroys the body's immune system and leads to death

anal sex – Inserting something (penis, sex toy, finger...) in the anus for sexual pleasure

anus – Butt hole

asshole – Slang for anus

balls – Slang for testicles

birth control – A method, device, or drug (or a combination of any of these), used with the intention of preventing pregnancy

bisexual – A person who is physically and emotionally attracted to both men and women

blow job – Slang for oral sex on a guy: using the mouth on the penis for pleasure

bollocks – British slang for testicles

cervix – The narrow lower part of a woman's uterus that has an opening that connects the uterus to the vagina

circumcision – The practice of removing the foreskin of the penis

clitoris (or "clit") – The female sex organ that is located between the labia at the upper end of the vulva; stimulation of it can make a girl have an orgasm

cojones – Spanish slang for testicles

condom – A thin tubular baggy that is made of latex or polyurethane and that covers the penis to catch all ejaculate fluid (pre-cum and cum)

consent – A person's voluntary agreement or permission to engage in sexual activity. Sexual activity without consent is sexual assault.

contraceptive – Something that prevents pregnancy (see "birth control")

cum (come) – Slang for ejaculation and/or semen; also slang for orgasm (male or female)

cunnilingus – The clinical word for oral sex on a girl; using the mouth/tongue on a woman's vagina for pleasure

cyber sex – Using the internet to exchange arousing or sexy messages with another person

dental dam – A thin piece of material that is silky and soft, to hold over the vagina or anus during oral sex to reduce the risk of sexually transmitted infections by stopping fluid exchange between partners

dick – Slang for penis

doggy style – Slang for a sexual position where one person is on their hands and knees and the other person penetrates them from behind

eating out – Slang for oral sex on a girl

ejaculation – When your penis squirts semen (cums) during an orgasm

embryo – A fertilized human egg before it grows into a fetus (at about 8 to 12 weeks after the sperm fertilized the egg)

erectile dysfunction – Being unable to get or keep an erection. Sometimes also called impotence.

erection – When a penis becomes stiff with added blood flow; caused by physical or mental stimulation

fallopian tube – Inside a woman's body, one of two narrow tubes through which an egg travels from an ovary to the uterus

fellatio – The clinical word for oral sex on a guy (blow job)

female condom – A polyurethane pouch worn by a woman during sex; it entirely lines the vagina and it helps prevent pregnancy and STIs including HIV

fetus – An embryo after it has taken the rough shape of a human (at about 8 to 12 weeks after the sperm fertilized the egg)

fingering – Slang for having intercourse using fingers, rather than a penis, in a partner's vagina or anus

foreplay – All the stuff that gets you excited before sex: flirting, touching, rubbing, kissing, etc.

foreskin – The loose flap of skin covering the end of the penis. Guys who have been circumcised no longer have a foreskin.

gay – Being physically and emotionally attracted to someone of the same sex

gender – The characteristics and behavior that society expects from a person based on that person's biological sex

go down – Slang meaning to give oral sex

G-spot – A small area on the front wall of the vagina that is especially sensitive to sexual stimulation in some women

hand job – Slang for rubbing a guy's penis by hand until he cums

hard-on – Slang for erection

head (giving head) – Slang meaning to give oral sex

heterosexual – Being physically and emotionally attracted to someone of the opposite sex

HIV – Human immunodeficiency virus: the virus that causes AIDS. It can be passed from an infected person through blood, semen (cum), vaginal fluids, or breast milk. Activities like unprotected sex and sharing needles are at a high risk for transmitting HIV.

homosexual – Being physically and emotionally attracted to someone of the same sex

hormones – Natural chemicals in your body that affect how your mind and body work. Men tend to have more of the hormone testosterone, and women tend to have more estrogen.

impotence – Being unable to get or keep an erection. Also called erectile dysfunction.

jerking off – Slang for masturbation

labia – The lips of the vagina

lesbian – A woman who is physically and emotionally attracted to other women

lube / lubricant – A water-based slippery substance used in sex to make things more comfortable and safe by reducing friction. Oil-based lubricants damage condoms and so should not be used.

masturbation – Touching oneself in a sexual manner for pleasure using fingers, sex toys, etc.

menstruation – A woman's period: the time of month that her uterus sheds its lining, and the blood and tissue comes out of her vagina. When a woman is pregnant, she does not have her period: the lining stays in the uterus to protect the fertilized egg.

missionary position – A sexual position where the woman lies on her back and the man lies on top facing her.

nuts – Slang for testicles

oral sex – Using your mouth and tongue on your partner's genitals to give sexual pleasure

orgasm – The feeling, during sex or masturbation, of great pleasure and release of pressure as muscles contract and then relax. With guys, this usually happens when you ejaculate semen. Women sometimes ejaculate too, but with a clear liquid, not semen.

ovaries – The organs inside a woman's body that release an egg once per month

ovulation – The point in a woman's menstrual cycle where her body releases an egg from an ovary into a fallopian tube. An egg fertilized with sperm results in pregnancy.

penis – The male sex organ

period – When a woman menstruates, meaning that the blood and tissue from the uterus come out through her vagina. This begins at puberty and then usually happens once per month and lasts a few days.

phone sex – Simulating sex by describing it to someone on the phone

Pill (the Pill) – Short for birth control pill; a pill taken daily by a woman to prevent pregnancy

prostate – A gland in your body, near the anus and bladder, that provides some of the liquid in semen

queer – Slang for being of a different sexuality than straight (heterosexual)

rimming – Slang for oral sex involving the tongue and anus

rectum – The area of the body just inside the anus

scrotum – The bag of skin between your legs that holds your testicles

semen – The white stuff that comes out of your penis when you ejaculate. It contains sperm, the male sex cells that combine with a woman's egg to make her pregnant.

sex toy – Any object that is designed and used to make sex fun and exciting

sexual assault – When someone is forced into any sexual act or has any sexual act forced upon them against their will

sixty-nine – Slang for a sexual position where both partners are able to give oral sex to each other at the same time

sphincter – A ring of muscles like the ones inside the anus (the anal sphincter)

sperm – The male reproductive cell that combines with a woman's egg to make her pregnant. The semen that you ejaculate contains millions of sperm.

spermicide – A gel that contains a chemical that kills sperm before it can fertilize a woman's egg. Spermicides can cause severe allergic reactions, irritation, or numbness so are generally best avoided.

STD – Sexually transmitted disease; also called sexually transmitted infection (STI)

STI – Sexually transmitted infection; also called sexually transmitted disease (STD)

straight – Slang for heterosexual

testicles – The oval-shaped organs in a guy's scrotum that produce sperm and testosterone

testosterone – The hormone that tells the body to grow characteristics we associate with guys, like facial hair, broad shoulders, and a deeper voice

transgendered – When a person feels that the gender they were assigned at birth does not reflect the gender they feel inside themselves

urethra – The tube inside your penis through which piss and semen travel, though not at the same time

uterus – The pear-shaped organ in a woman's body that is designed to hold and nourish a fertilized egg as it grows from embryo to fetus to a baby ready for birth. The narrow lower part of the uterus becomes the cervix, a canal that connects to the vagina.

vagina – A woman's internal genitals: the tunnel that begins between the legs of a woman and leads inside her body to the cervix and uterus

vaginal sex – Penetration of the vagina for sexual gratification by fingers, penis, sex toys, etc.

wet dream – A sexy dream that causes you to ejaculate while you are sleeping

whack off – Slang for masturbation

About St. Stephen's Community House and the Youth Arcade Program

St. Stephen's Community House is a unique, community-based social service agency that has been serving the needs of Kensington Market and surrounding neighborhoods in downtown West Toronto since 1962.

Operating with a staff of over 150 people and with the support of almost 400 volunteers, we provide services for more than 32,000 people a year. St. Stephen's addresses the most pressing issues in its community—poverty, hunger, homelessness, unemployment, isolation, conflict and violence, AIDS, racism, youth alienation, and the integration of refugees and immigrants.

Specifically, we will endeavor to maintain and to enhance our role as a leader and partner in the community by providing:
- A quick response to community needs
- Access to a range of services for children, youth, adults, and seniors
- Immigrant and refugee support programs
- Advocacy to improve the quality of life of our community
- Support for community capacity building
- Effective, high impact programs

THE YOUTH ARCADE'S MISSION: To provide a range of youth services that (1) meet emerging and critical youth social, health, recreation, and education needs; (2) empower youth to speak, advocate, and lead youth programming that impacts on their lives; (3) assist youth facing a range of barriers and life experiences through the transition to young adulthood safely and confidently; (4) encourage youth to think critically about themselves and the community in which they live.

How do we make sense of our mission? The Arcade has become the hub of the youth community in our neighborhoods. Youth know it to be a place where they can get information in a non-judgmental and supportive environment. Parents know it's a safe place where their kids can hang out and socialize with their peers while getting information and support. In addition, the Arcade programs are designed to assist youth make the transition from being a teenager to a young adult. Programs support our youth educational endeavors, support their social skills and learning, develop their leadership skills, and build resilience. Funders know it as a well-managed, youth-driven program with strong community networks. St. Stephen's Community House and the Youth Arcade receive on-going financial support from the City of Toronto and the United Way of Greater Toronto.

ACKNOWLEDGMENTS

First, we at St. Stephen's Community House would like to thank all the young men who participated in the creation of this book. Whether you were involved in the ongoing after-school candid conversations, performing research, producing writing, creating artwork, doing healthy sexuality workshops, or assisting with layout and organization of the product, you were all integral to making this book possible.

A special thank you to Andrew Coimbra for all his dedication and enthusiasm, creative genius, and honesty that helped us shape the nature of this book.

A big thanks goes out to Gordon McLean who was the original facilitator of the group of young men producing the book and who put in countless hours and brought incredible passion and commitment to the process.

An ongoing thank you to Marlon Merraro, the previous Manager of the Youth Services at St. Stephen's Community House. Marlon truly inspired and challenged every young man who participated in this process. He challenged them to think more critically, to evaluate their ideas and values, to understand the implications of their actions, and to grow to be strong and proud of who they are in order to become all they can be.

Thank you to David Wichman who worked alongside of the young men ensuring that their ideas and stories came to life in this book, and who took on the editing of the materials which was not an easy challenge.

Thank you to the numerous Youth Arcade funders and especially Toronto Public Health, who funded us for the initial stages of creating this book, for supporting young people in creating their own educational resources.

A huge thanks to all the Youth Arcade staff for the ongoing work ensuring that young people have access to the information needed to become healthy and vibrant adults and for being so intensely committed to our youth community and the issues they face. A special thanks to St. Stephen's Community House for their 20 year commitment to maintaining a vibrant youth program that contributes to creating opportunities for young men and women.

ANNICK PRESS ACKNOWLEDGMENTS

Annick Press would like to thank the following individuals for contributing to and/or reviewing the manuscript and offering their professional input:

Cathy Maser, *RN, MN, Paediatric Nurse Practitioner, Division of Adolescent Medicine, The Hospital for Sick Children, Toronto*

Dr. Rahul Saxena, *MD, MSc, FRCPC, FAAP, Staff Paediatrician, Division of Adolescent Medicine, Hospital for Sick Children, Toronto*

Leighann Wichman, *Executive Director, Youth Project, Halifax*

INDEX

abortion 212–13, 218–19
  See also pregnancy and options
abstinence 89, 111
  See also relationships; sex and
  sexual tastes
abuse. *See* consent; relationships;
  violence
adoption 213–15
  See also pregnancy and options
age and puberty. *See* puberty
age and consent 120.
  See also consent
age and relationships 77, 118–19
AIDS (acquired immune deficiency
  syndrome). *See* HIV and AIDS
anal sex 107–109. *See also* lubrication; sex and sexual tastes; STIs
arguments. *See* relationships

balls. *See* testicles and scrotum
birth control 185–211
  and myths about 187–90
  cervical cap 204
  condoms 187, 200, 206–208.
    See also condoms
  contraceptive patch 201–202
  diaphragm 203
  emergency contraceptive pill
    (ECP) 209–11
  female condoms 200–201
  injection (Depo-Provera) 201
  IUD (intrauterine device) 203
  IUS (intrauterine system,
    Mirena) 203–204
  monthly charting 205
  nuva ring 202

Pill (the Pill, oral contraceptive)
    187, 199
  spermicide 204. *See also*
    nonoxynol-9
  sponge 204
  tubal ligation 205
  vasectomy 204–205
  See also pregnancy and options
bisexual. *See* gay or bisexual
blow job. *See* oral sex
blue balls 23. *See also* testicles
breaking up. *See* relationships

cervical cap. *See* birth control
cheating. *See* relationships
chlamydia. *See* STIs
circumcision. *See* penis
coming out. *See* gay or bisexual
communication. *See* consent;
    relationships
condoms (male condoms) 103,
    104–105, 140–42, 143–44,
    206–208
  See also birth control;
    dental dam; female condom,
    HIV/AIDS; lubrication; STIs
consensual age. *See* consent
consent 78, 128, 130–32
  age of consent 120
  See also drinking and drugs
contraception. *See* birth control
contraceptive patch. *See* birth
    control
cum. *See* penis; sex and sexual
    tastes; wet dreams

dental dams 103, 148, 149, 151
Depo-Provera (injection). *See* birth
    control

diaphragm. *See* birth control
drinking and drugs 12, 124–129
drugs. *See* drinking and drugs

eating out. *See* oral sex
emergency contraceptive pill (ECP).
    See birth control
erections 4, 9–10, 23
    problems with erections 11–12,
    15, 124, 126, 127
    See also sex and sexual tastes

female anatomy. *See* pregnancy
    and options
female condoms. *See* birth control
first time 88, 90–93, 137, 190

gay or bisexual 48–51, 98–99, 190
    coming out 54–60
    See also gender norms;
    homophobia; relationships; sex
    and sexual tastes; transgender
gender norms 61–62, 63
genital herpes. *See* STIs
gonorrhea. *See* STIs

hard ons. *See* erections
hepatitis B. *See* STIs
HIV and AIDS. *See also* STIs
    139, 156–57, 166–70, 171–72,
    176, 177, 178-83
    HIV treatment 177
homophobia 51, 98–99
    See also gay or bisexual
HPV (human papilloma virus).
    See STIs

injection (Depo-Provera). *See* birth
    control
IUD (intrauterine device). *See* birth
    control
IUS (intrauterine system, Mirena).
    See birth control

jealousy. *See* relationships

lubrication 105–106, 108
    See also condoms; sex and
    sexual tastes

masturbation 23, 24, 25, 83–84,
    85, 100
    See also sex and sexual tastes
menstruation (woman's period)
    189, 196–197
    See also birth control
monthly charting. *See* birth control

needle use. *See* STIs
nocturnal emission. *See* wet dreams
nonoxynol-9 103, 104
numbing 103, 104
nuva ring. *See* birth control

oral contraceptive (the Pill).
    See birth control
oral sex 102–104. *See also* sex
    and sexual tastes
orgasm. *See* sex and sexual tastes

parenting. *See* pregnancy and
   options
penis 1–2, 4, 7–18
   circumcised 17–18
   uncircumcised 15, 17–18
   hygiene 15–16, 17–18
   penis size 7–8
   See also erections.
periods. *See* menstruation
Pill (the Pill, oral contraceptive).
   See birth control
pornography 121–23
pre-cum 13-14
   See also penis
pregnancy and options 212–22
   abortion 212–13, 218–19
   adoption 213–15
   birth control. *See* birth control
   conception, how pregnancy
   happens 191–97
   parenting 215–16, 220-22
   pregnancy scare 70, 88
puberty 3–4, 24
   onset of 3, 5
   delays in 5–6
   signs of 3–4
pubic lice (crabs). *See* STIs

relationships 27, 29–79, 173–75
   age and relationships 77;
      see also age of consent
   arguments 68, 77
   abuse and violence 35, 75, 79
   breaking up 72–73
   cheating 35, 66–67, 78
   communication 29–33, 37,
      68-69, 72, 76, 78
   gay or bisexual 48, 49-60
   healthy 31, 65, 70, 76–77
   jealousy 34, 64

unhealthy 34–35, 36, 65, 75, 76
   See also sex and sexual tastes

scabies. *See* STIs
scrotum. *See* testicles and scrotum
semen 4, 14, 24, 85
   See also penis; sex and sexual
   tastes; birth control
sex and sexual tastes 81–135,
      173–75
   abstinence 89, 111
   anal sex 105, 107–109
   and drinking and drugs 124–129
   first time 88, 90-93, 137, 190
   G-spot 115
   kissing 86–87
   lubrication 105–106, 109
   masturbation 83-84, 85
   oral sex 102–104
   orgasm 112–15
   pornography 121–23
   sex toys 108
   vaginal sex 105, 110, 114, 115
   See also birth control; consent;
   HIV and AIDS; relationships; STIs
sexual assault. *See* consent;
   violence
spermicide. *See* birth control;
   condoms
sponge. *See* birth control
STD (sexually transmitted disease).
   See STI
STIs (sexually transmitted infections)
      16, 22, 137–142, 145–83
   and oral sex 102–104, 137
   chlamydia 139, 147–48
   genital herpes 139, 152–54
   gonorrhea 149–50
   hepatitis B 139, 154–55
   HIV and AIDS. *See* HIV and AIDS

HPV (human papilloma virus)
158–59
pubic lice (crabs) 159–61
scabies 161–62
syphilis 139, 150–52
trichomoniasis 163
syphilis. *See* STIs

tattoos. *See* STIs
testicles and scrotum 19–23
transgender 61–62, 63
trichomoniasis. *See* STIs
tubal ligation. *See* birth control

vaginal sex. *See* sex and sexual
tastes
vasectomy. *See* birth control
violence 35, 75, 79, 130–32.
See also abuse; consent;
relationships.
virginity. *See* first time

wet dreams 24, 25